Additional Praise for *Beyond Church Walls*

"What often passes for 'pastoral care' in many churches is a degradation of truly, peculiarly, mission-driven pastoral care. Rick Rouse connects our care with our leadership of a church that realizes we can only be faithful by being the church beyond the walls of the church, joining in Christ's active embrace of his beloved Creation. Rouse calls us forward to truly Christian pastoral care."

Will Willimon, Duke Divinity School

"An experienced pastor and well-formed guide, Rick Rouse aims to help us navigate the shifting place of the church in relation to culture and context. Drawing together scripture, theology, and the practical wisdom found in ministry stories and strategies, this work's clear purpose is to imagine congregations turned toward care for the larger communities of which they are a part. Pastors and congregational leaders will find here a lively vison for the church acting out what it celebrates in its worship: Jesus Christ, the generosity of God for each and every one—for this whole wide world."

Thomas H. Schattauer, Wartburg Theological Seminary

"Rick Rouse has reframed congregational care from the pastor taking care of the congregation, to the congregation caring for the community. Beyond Church Walls explores care ministry for the outwardly-focused church."

Michael Rinehart, bishop, Texas–Louisiana Gulf Coast Synod Evangelical Lutheran Church in America

Beyond Church Walls

Sue —

Blessings on your journey of grace!

Beyond Church Walls

Cultivating a Culture of Care

Rick Rouse

Fortress Press
Minneapolis

BEYOND CHURCH WALLS

Cultivating a Culture of Care

Cover image: Calvary Lutheran, South Minneapolis. Photo by Rick Rouse.

Cover design: Alisha Lofgren

Library of Congress Cataloging-in-Publication Data

Print ISBN: 978-1-4514-9034-3

ebook ISBN: 978-1-5064-1027-2

The paper used in this publication meets the minimum requirements of American National Standard for Information Sciences — Permanence of Paper for Printed Library Materials, ANSI Z329.48-1984.

Manufactured in the U.S.A.

This book was produced using Pressbooks.com, and PDF rendering was done by PrinceXML.

To our children, Michael, Nicole, and Ryan
who bring joy and give us hope for the future

"While not everyone can do great things, we all can do small things with great love."
—*Mother Teresa of Calcutta*

Contents

Acknowledgments

Thank you to Mary Sue Dreier and her students at Lutheran Theological Southern Seminary for field testing parts of this book. Special thanks to Jessicah Krey Duckworth for writing the Preface and to Thomas Schattauer of Wartburg Theological Seminary for contributing liturgies of life transitions.

Foreword

Jessicah Krey Duckworth

A job title has an incredible way of informing one's work. When I taught at Luther Seminary in St. Paul, Minnesota, my title was Assistant Professor of Congregational and Community Care Leadership, and the department in which I taught carried the same name. The title begged for explanation. Why congregational care? Because care is the responsibility of the whole congregation. Why community? Because the community members and organizations in which a congregation is located also carry the responsibility to provide care for the neighbors who call a community home. *How* a congregation interfaces with the community's care and vice versa is a question worth engaging. The twofold vision created by my job title provided an opportunity for me and the students in each classroom of learning to reimagine our inclinations and expectations about the field and practice of pastoral care.

How might the church's caring activities participate in God's vision for healing and redemption of the world? For whom ought the body of Christ to care? How does a missional perspective motivate a congregation's commitment to care beyond the church and how does care motivate mission? These questions arose among the participants in the classes I taught at Luther. And these are the normative questions Rick Rouse invites congregations to explore throughout the pages of this book, *Beyond Church Walls*. Here he lays out a vision for congregations who would consider cultivating a culture of care in response to God's missional calling.

Though the capacity for a wider circle of care exists in every community, many congregations are not well informed to provide such care, theologically or practically. Most congregations have processes set up to care for established members. Rouse describes a missional perspective of pastoral care that extends the caregiving role beyond the pastor's or congregational leader's responsibility to the whole congregation, and further, extends the congregation's care beyond established members toward people and partners within the community beyond the walls of the church. Congregation and community care motivates congregations to attend to the needs of their surrounding community and seek to build partnerships with community organizations already providing good care. In this model, *where* care is happening is as important as *who* is caring. A missional perspective of pastoral care invites a congregation's leadership to nurture and support the caring relationships within the congregation and between the congregation and community. Care is hope made visible in the world God loves.

This perspective wells up from within Rouse's own experience as a pastor. In August 1992, his congregation's building was burned to the ground by a serial arsonist. In Christian love and care, Pastor Rouse and his congregation reached out to the family of the arsonist, and to the community surrounding the church. What was the result of this gracious outreach? A new church building designed as a community center to partner with and host the community in shared efforts to care for one another in light of the good news of God's compassion and hope. In this book, Rouse blends his passion for discipleship and evangelism with his wisdom around building a missional, caring community. He writes about the convictions he lives.

The call of the missional church is to proclaim gospel as good news for the human condition, to confess hope in action as concretely as possible—a hope made visible in Jesus' ministry. As Jesus provided care and forgiveness to all he encountered, so too the church is called to seek the welfare of all of creation. As such, a missional church seeks to align its ministries of care with God's good news of compassion and hope for the whole world.

I imagine you picked up this book because like me, you love the church and yet, have a sense that the love and care shared within the church is needed in large measure beyond the church as well. In your hands you have a resource to inspire that hope into a reality.

Introduction

All who believed were together and had all things in common; they would sell their possessions and goods, and distribute the proceeds to all, as any had need. Day by day, as they spent much time together in the temple, they broke bread at home and ate their food with glad and generous hearts, praising God and having the goodwill of all the people. And day by day the Lord added to their number those who were being saved. (Acts 2:44-47)

When Christianity Makes an Impact

There are several significant actions in this passage that describe the nature of the early church. Striking among them are: 1) they would sell their possessions and distribute to all in need, 2) they had the goodwill of all the general population, and 3) they attracted new believers and the church grew. It is the premise of the author that this is a Missional model for pastoral care and possible church growth.

It is told by historians in the first century that citizens of the empire would remark: "See those Christians and how they love others." The early believers practiced an ethic of love and care for all people, not just their own. In a culture that left the widow, orphan, and disabled to care for themselves, they selected members of their faith community called deacons to provide care for the unfortunate. In many ways, this was the beginning of the first social service movement. This is one of the reasons that Christianity grew like wildfire during the first three centuries, in spite of persecution by the Roman government. Christians were known for practicing a different lifestyle, living by a higher standard suggested by Jesus when he called his followers to love others and be servants of all.

> The works of charity that Christians accomplished in the Roman Empire continue to be one of the greatest stars in the Church's crown. . . . Hospitality to strangers was important in a day when inns were not desirable places. Ancient society did not provide care for orphans but allowed them to be raised for prostitution or other disreputable occupations. Christians made these unfortunates the object of their concern. Since the only hospitals in existence were private or associated with religious cults, Christians also took care of the sick. During plagues in Carthage and Alexandria around the middle of the third century, the Christians cared for the suffering even after the pagans had abandoned them.[1]

One can cite examples throughout history where this pattern of community care was followed by a rise in the number of conversions to the Christian faith. It was the church that responded to the early plagues, caring for the sick and burying the dead. Following World War II, it was Lutheran World Relief that brought comfort to many of the victims of war by providing food and shelter throughout Europe and in the United States as well. Churches swelled in numbers during the late forties and throughout the fifties, in part because of this kind of community outreach. In present-day China, the Protestant Church there has been the one to provide AIDS education and medicine, establish health clinics in rural areas, and build nursing homes to care for an aging population. The result has been a dramatic increase in the number of new Christians. In light of these examples, we are compelled to ask: *"How do congregations of today relate to social issues, economic injustice, and the political leaders of the day and how can that make a difference?"*

The Perfect Storm

We are facing enormous cultural shifts and challenges in the USA. From 1990 to 2010, those who identified themselves as Christian dropped from 86 percent to 69 percent. At the present rate of change, some believe most Americans will be non-Christians by the year 2035. While 50 percent of those over forty-five attend church, fewer than 30 percent of those under forty-five attend. Just one-third of adults in their twenties and thirties claim to be committed Christians. Yet 80 percent of them claim that religion or spirituality is important in their life.[2]

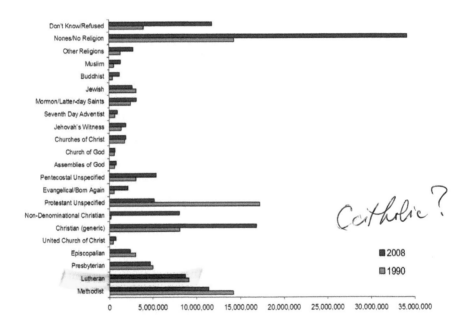

The NONE category now far eclipses all the other religious groups in the US.[3] In her book *Belief Without Borders*, Linda Mercadante reports that there are now more NONES in America than all the Protestants put together. She cites statistics that between 1990 and 2000 the number doubled from 14.3 to 29.4 million. And by 2010,

46 million or 20 percent of all Americans had no religious affiliation.[4] Why are they shunning organized religion?

Let's look at a study of the beliefs of the NONES; this includes all ages of those who are unaffiliated, not associated with any religious organization. 1. Religious people are hypocritical, judgmental, and insincere. 2. Religions are partly true, but none are completely true. 3. Religious organizations are too focused on rules, not spirituality. 4. Religious leaders only want money and power. 5. Religious people are anti-science.[5]

Linda Mercadante has studied the beliefs of the NONES or unaffiliated and shares her conclusions. She indicates that the largest percentage is among young adults, estimating that as many as three-quarters of them identify in this category. She indicates that young people are now more religiously unaffiliated than earlier generations were at the same age. It cannot be denied that "a growing number of Americans have ceased to identify with, contribute to, or remain devoted to any particular religious tradition or faith community."[6]

She goes on to say that while this trend may seem to indicate we are becoming more secular in America, something else may be happening instead. A significant number of NONES are looking to develop their own spirituality apart from traditional structures. Spirituality tends to refer to the interior life of faith without the trappings of organized religion. She concludes that we are in a time of widespread openness to spiritual things and a new willingness to sacrifice time, money, and effort to find a connection to something larger than ourselves. What is important to these seekers is that belief, experience, and behavior go together. Most agree that to be authentic and to have integrity, one should be living out what one believes. Churches would do well to model the early Christians in the Book of Acts by serving the needs of their surrounding communities, providing care for those in need if they are to reflect this authenticity.[7]

PROJECTING NORTH AMERICA:
Christian growth slows, 'Nones' soar

Christians	"Nones"	Jews	2050 pop.
65.8%	25.6%	1.4%	435,420,000
(77.4% in 2010)	(17.1% in 2010)	(1.8% in 2010)	(+26.4% from 2010)

© 2015 Religion News Service. Graphic by Tiffany McCallen
SOURCE: Pew Research Center, "The Future of World Religions:
Population Growth Projections 2010-2050"

The changing religious and spiritual landscape calls for a major paradigm shift in the way we understand the role and task of the local congregation. Church leaders need to wake up before it is too late; they must seek to be in mission rather than in maintenance if they are to make an impact on their neighborhoods and the wider world. They need to realize the church is the only organization that exists for reasons other than its own self-preservation.

There are two bodies of water in Israel. One is the Dead Sea, so called because there is no outlet for the water it receives. It only takes, so cannot sustain life. The other is the Sea of Galilee, teeming with life and emptying into the Jordan River and giving nourishment to the land. As a church we are to exemplify the latter. Jesus calls us to give ourselves away in love for the sake of the world.

An Expanded Definition of Pastoral Care

Today's missional frontier is challenging, transforming, and reinvigorating. There are many exciting stories about Christians and congregations with new and renewed energy for God's mission. Our understanding has been informed and inspired by the growing number of church leaders and literature addressing this new era of mission. The author has worked alongside other pastors, lay leaders, and seminary students who are also developing a new missional imagination. We have seen how congregations and church structures are adapting in this time of unprecedented change and opportunity. Yet, one important area of congregational activity has been undeveloped and, in many cases, overlooked: the relationship between the renewed missional calling of the church and the tradition of pastoral care.

Pastoral care has been traditionally understood as pastoral acts administered to individuals or small groups—usually within congregations or church-related institutions—by an ordained or lay religious practitioner. As congregations in the twenty-first century begin to reclaim the missional nature of the church, this view must be broadened to also include care and concern for the needs of the larger community. A *missional perspective* does not diminish or abandon the fine traditions of pastoral care, but engages them within this wider perspective. A *missional perspective* believes that good pastoral care leads to mission and that mission is undergirded by good pastoral care. A *missional perspective* of pastoral care embraces the notion that all of God's people—not just trained professionals—are called to partner in God's healing and redemption of the world. A *missional perspective* sees pastoral care and mission as inseparable.

This book is designed to assist pastors and church leaders in assessing their congregation's readiness for mission in the form of community care and making the cultural shift from membership to discipleship. The first chapter will focus on reclaiming God's vision for the church as a partner in the healing and redemption of the world, as we seek to expand the definition of pastoral care that includes God's missional imperative. Chapter two reflects on the changing paradigm for pastoral care in the twenty-first century within a biblical and theological framework. Chapter three deals with the challenges of change and how congregations might begin to cultivate a *culture of care*. Chapters four and five look at *contexts of care* and *components of care*—considering where and how congregations create communities of care. Chapter six offers guidelines for developing a congregational approach to community organization. Chapter seven discusses the power of ritual to bring healing and transformation to individuals and communities. Finally, chapter eight provides some practical guidelines for mapping congregational assets, strategic planning, and developing a vision for mission.

The following are key questions I have tried to address and encourage congregations to wrestle with. *What are the gifts God brings to communities through missional pastoral care? And how will we adapt our practices to participate in God's mission?* All of this leads us to explore in this book what the relationship is between pastoral care and the "Missional Call" of the congregation. And, finally, what does it mean to adopt a new definition of pastoral care that includes care for the community around us?

Notes

1. Edward A. Engelbrecht, ed., *The Church from Age to Age* (St. Louis: Concordia, 2011), 58–59.
2. Kenneth Inskeep, ELCA Research and Evaluation, Trend Report for 1990–2010.

3. Ibid.

4. Linda Mercadante, *Belief Without Borders: Inside the Minds of the Spiritual but Not Religious* (New York: Oxford University Press, 2014), 1.

5. Kenneth Inskeep, Report to Covenant Cluster, February 20–22, 2014.

6. Mercadante, *Belief Without Borders*, 2.

7. Religion News Service: http://religionnews.com/2015/04/02/future-map-religions-reveals-world-change-christians-muslims-jews/.

1

Reclaiming God's Vision for Community Care

Where there is no vision the people perish. (Proverbs 29:18)

I was pastor of Trinity Lutheran Church in the Greater Seattle area when a six-month arson spree began. Our congregation was one of the first victims and our church campus was totally destroyed. The metropolitan area was terrorized as churches, businesses, and homes were burned. Six months later, a young man by the name of Paul Keller was arrested and charged with over a hundred counts of arson. While there had been some copycat arsonists, Paul pled guilty to about seventy counts of arson.

I was surprised to read in the paper that it was Paul because I had worked with him and his dad's advertising agency to plan a publicity campaign for the local churches. The next day I went to the Snohomish County jail in Everett, Washington to visit him. Paul was surprised to see me and exclaimed: "Pastor, I can't believe you've come. Not after all the heartache I've caused you and your congregation." And then he added: "I've been sober now for the first time in months and have been reading my Bible. I wonder if God can ever forgive me because I don't think I can ever forgive myself."

I reminded Paul that he was a baptized child of God and that God looked at him through the cross of Jesus Christ. I said, "God forgives you, loves you, and God still has a plan for your life." Then I explained that while I couldn't speak for the congregation, I forgave him and would pray for him. At that Paul broke down; he wept and he wept. He then asked if he could write a letter of apology to our congregation, which I read at worship the following Sunday. The leadership of Trinity responded in kind by drafting a letter offering their forgiveness, prayers, and support for Paul and his family. That was the beginning of a unique relationship between the congregation, the Keller family, and the greater community.

We invited the victims of arson to join our congregation and Paul's family to come together for a service of forgiveness and healing. Then throughout the days leading up to Paul's sentencing and beyond, Trinity sought to be an agent of healing and reconciliation. The incident helped redefine how we saw ourselves and our mission. We embraced God's vision for ministry by choosing to embody Christ's call to bring healing to a hurting world. A new vision statement was adopted: "Through Christ: healing hurts, restoring hope, and rebuilding dreams."

One powerful example was a Valentine's Day luncheon held at a neighboring church, as we were still without a building. Paul Keller's dad had turned in his son and so received a $25,000 reward from the arson task force. George Keller didn't feel right in accepting the money for himself after all the damage his son had caused in the community, so offered it to our congregation. The leaders of Trinity decided to use the funds to provide grants to various community and religious agencies who were involved in some kind of healing ministry, such as the Fire Fighters Fund for Victims, the local women's shelter, and Lutheran Community Services. Representatives from all the organizations who had applied were at the luncheon. And as I read their names, they came forward to receive their grant check. George and Margaret Keller, Paul's parents, were there to hand *it to them and shake their hands. In some cases they received a hug from the grateful recipient. There wasn't a dry eye in the house.*

Trinity chose to build not just a new church but a community center that would continue to be a "mission outpost" committed to providing healing and hope for people in the larger community. Their witness to the gospel became widely known throughout the state of Washington and across the country through various news media. Today the congregation is home to a number of social service agencies and community outreach programs. People from all over the Puget Sound region are attracted to its ministry and it has become one of the largest Lutheran congregations in the Northwest Washington Synod of the Evangelical Lutheran Church in America.[1]

Trinity embraced God's vision for a new, missional future. The congregation looked outside of itself as it contemplated what God was up to and where God might be leading them. They had recently celebrated fifty years of ministry in their north Seattle neighborhood and then lost their entire campus. Yet they were able to look beyond the tragedy of the fire to discern what God's purpose was for them in this day and time, and discovered how they could be God's instrument of healing and reconciliation for others in the larger community.

This chapter invites congregations to consider what it means to partner with God in mission and reclaim God's vision of ministry for the sake of the world. We will explore what is meant by *missio Dei*—God's mission plan—and how congregations are invited to participate in making the reign of God more visible in their communities. We will reflect on biblical and theological concepts such as the relational nature of God as Trinity and what it means to live simultaneously in "two kingdoms" as we seek to understand how to be a "church for others" in the twenty-first century.

What Is God's Mission Plan?

Knowing why the church exists and what difference a congregation is making in the world is a key indicator for motivation, impact, and growth. Congregations where members have little understanding about what their purpose is—why God has planted them in a particular ministry context—tend to generate little enthusiasm, passion, and support. Without a vision for mission, God's people lack direction and face an uncertain future. What the writer of Proverbs suggests may ring true for many church communities: "Where there is no vision, the people perish." Today churches of all denominations are closing their doors at an alarming rate.

It is not enough for congregations to develop a mission statement and then invite God to bless it. Congregations often forget that it is God who has a mission, the *missio Dei,* and congregations exist to help carry out that mission. Congregations are invited to partner with God in God's mission plan for the healing and redemption of the world. The missional congregation understands that it is primarily a missional community of people being trained and equipped to live among the world as daily disciples of Jesus.

God had a plan for the church from the very beginning. It was to be a vessel for the gospel of God's grace in Jesus Christ. It was to be a church for others. Ministry was not just intended to nurture and strengthen the faithful, for the church was called to give itself away for the sake of the world. The early church had mission outposts that were eventually called congregations. These congregations carried out God's work of love and care in the world in a variety of ways. Today we would define a *missional congregation* as one that connects their ministry with what God is up to in the world.

Connection is the operative word. To be in mission assumes that a congregation desires to connect with the outside world. To do so the church must overcome the challenge of isolation, trapped in a world limited to their own perspectives and suspicious of others. Joel Hunter believes that "the church has grown more and more isolated over the years as it has withdrawn more and more into itself. . . . That kind of isolation in the church started with its institutionalization after the conversion of Emperor Constantine in A.D. 312. Given the power to distance itself from the attacks from outside, and to jettison disagreements on the inside, the church began building walls."[2]

Congregations are being called to move beyond the walls of the church that have served to protect and isolate them from their neighbors. It takes courage to move beyond one's comfort zone and enter the brave new world of God's mission field. Consider how Broadway Methodist Church in Indianapolis risked everything to follow God's leading in caring for their community. Led by Pastor Mike Mather, they abandoned their traditional charity work and redefined what it means to serve in an urban community. They began to see their neighbors as children of God.

Broadway UMC's leaders have changed the way they view their neighbors—as people with gifts, not just needs. In what ways does this view reframe the conversation? What difference does reframing the relationship make in the outcomes achieved? "The church, and me in particular," Mather said, "has done a lot of work where we have treated the people around us as if, at worst, they are a different species and, at best, as if they are people to be pitied and helped by us."

With that in mind, Broadway has—for more than a decade now—been reorienting itself. Rather than a bestower of blessings, the church is aiming to be something more humble. "The church decided its call was to be good neighbors. And that we should listen and see people as children of God," said De'Amon Harges, a church member who sees Broadway's transformation in terms not unlike Christ's death, burial, and resurrection . . .

Tamara Leech, an associate professor at the Indiana University Fairbanks School of Public Health, has been studying what Broadway is doing for the past six years. Social cohesion, Leech said, is a key to improving life in what she calls neighborhoods of the concentrated disadvantaged. "The neighbors see Broadway as a place where you can go and ask for help. Not for goods or services," she said. "You go there for connections."

Change also is evident in what's going on in Sunday school classrooms that sat dark for decades. Today, they are filled with an unusual collection of small businesses that rent space, together with fledgling organizations that get space for free. Meeting in the church now is a metropolitan youth orchestra and an eclectic mix of artists and, on Sunday nights, fifty or more gamers. There's a dance studio and a pottery shop and an office for a small architectural firm. The church acquired a commercial kitchen license, and now people from the neighborhood use it for catering startups.

Church staff member Cathy Pilarski, a onetime doubter, is in charge of managing all this. She still thinks her pastor is crazy. "Certifiable," she said, joking. But in each busy corner of the church, in each of the hundreds of faces that now pass under its roof each week, she sees something that was missing for a long time—the majesty of God. "I want to make sure that God is glorified not only in that sanctuary but in every corner of this building," she said. Some of that bustle has spilled over into the sanctuary. Sunday-morning attendance has climbed past 200. But in the Broadway economy, that's almost an afterthought.

Broadway has died to its old self, giving up the things that were holding it back, said Harges, the roving listener (whose job is to pay attention to the needs and gifts of the neighbors). The church's resurrection has come from seeking the gifts of others. "Our role in this place is to become like yeast—that invisible agent for social change. It is not about us as an agency inviting people to witness God here. Instead, what we want to do is to see God out of this place."[3]

The Trinity: A Relational Way of Being Church

God's mission is all about building relationships with others. Rather than being self-centered and preoccupied with themselves, congregations are encouraged to reach out to others. By nature, our triune God models what it means to be relationship-centered. Our three-in-one God is made manifest in the persons of Father, Son, and Holy Spirit. God desires that the church as the body of Christ replicate this divine nature by interacting with the world around it. Congregations are called to work through outside relationships, not just inside programs.[4]

The church by God's design is both transcendent and relational. As seen by the illustration below, the Christian faith likewise can be described as being both vertical and horizontal. One could say that the church has "cross purposes," with the vertical arm of the cross connecting it with God's love and grace, and the horizontal arm inviting God's people into relationship with others. In some ways, the cross below reflects the fourfold purpose of the church as it lives out its God-given mission in the world.

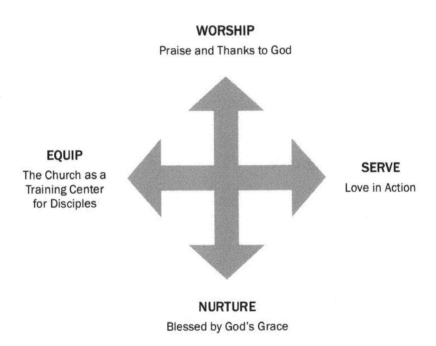

WORSHIP
Praise and Thanks to God

EQUIP
The Church as a
Training Center
for Disciples

SERVE
Love in Action

NURTURE
Blessed by God's Grace

Nurture comes from spiritual practices such as reading and hearing the Word of God. We discover God's grace poured out through love and forgiveness in the person of Jesus Christ. In response, God's people praise God in worship, offering thanksgiving for all that God has done. In worship we rejoice in the new creation that one becomes through baptism, and how that gift of new life is renewed in the celebration of the Eucharist. This leads God's people from the vertical to the horizontal, as they seek to be equipped as disciples of Jesus. Finally, living lives of service, they live out their baptism by loving and caring for others.

The church is called to reflect the image of the triune God by connecting with others. As Jesus sent the disciples, so God sends the church out into the world. "Understanding the Triune God as a sending God is foundational for understanding how the church is called and sent to participate in God's mission in the world. This perspective understands that the Triune God is intimately involved with the created world. The Triune God is a God that both creates and redeems. . . . God sent the Son into the world to accomplish redemption, and the Father and the Son continue to send the Spirit into the world to create the church and lead it into participation in God's mission."[5]

Sharing in the Reign of God

Jesus raised quite a ruckus in Nazareth the day he preached on a text from Isaiah. "The Spirit of the Lord is upon me, because he has anointed me to bring good news to the poor. He has sent me to proclaim release to the captives and recovery of sight to the blind, to let the oppressed go free, to proclaim the year of the Lord's favor."[6] The worshipers were scandalized when Jesus dared to suggest that he was the fulfillment of this prophecy. He had come to usher in the year of God's favor, God's reign of grace for all people.

Congregations need to be reminded that God sent the church into the world to be a visible sign of the reign of God, that is, to be agents of peace, justice, and love. From the days of the early church, the church was called to be countercultural, often standing over and against the dominant culture. The church was called to follow the example of Jesus in standing with and serving the poor, the disenfranchised, and those on the margins of society. In a culture of greed, the church was called to be generous in giving itself away for the sake of others. In a culture of exclusion, racism, and domination over those who were different or of a lower order, the church was called to be an inclusive community that encouraged equality and welcomed all in the name of Jesus. They sought to live out the truth of what St. Paul preached: "There is no longer Jew or Greek, there is no longer slave or free, there is no longer male and female; for all of you are one in Christ Jesus."[7] The church continues to be called to live out this truth in our world today.

The following illustration is evidence of one congregation's attempt to share the reign of God through their outreach ministry in the larger community and how their efforts multiplied.

It's 7 p.m. on a weeknight at a strip mall in Huntington Beach, California, and people have been lined up for hours outside a laundromat here. They've been waiting for a chance to do their wash for free. As they file in, volunteers direct them to the machines and help them to supplies. This is "Laundry Love" at work—a ministry that raises money to pay for detergent, dryer sheets, and quarters for machines.

Laundry is a daunting chore for many people, but for the working poor, the cost of doing laundry—not to mention the time involved in hauling it to a laundromat—can be prohibitive. It can also mean going without other basic essentials. Laundry Love gatherings may be the only time some people are able to wash their clothes, says volunteer Ken Kawamura.

The idea for Laundry Love began at an Episcopal congregation in Ventura, California, and slowly but surely, it's spreading. Now, more than seventy churches, mosques, and synagogues around the country have adopted the practice.

For Giovanna Cortez, Laundry Love has become a necessity. With three kids, she has lots of laundry—and she lost her job in March. "I have to come because I have no money for laundry," Cortez says. She says she probably saved fifty dollars last month by using the Laundry Love service.

Shannon Kassoff, one of the organizers of Laundry Love in Huntington Beach, says it's about more than just free laundry. This group was formed by people who became disillusioned with traditional church, and started taking over this Laundromat once a month.

"This is our church," Kassoff says. "It is probably the best way to be involved in other people's lives, not just handing out food in a soup kitchen, or whatever. We get to know them very well, and that's probably the best part of this whole deal."

David Clarke echoes that sentiment. Clarke never thought he would be on the receiving end of charity, until he lost his job as an aerospace machinist several years ago. He's been struggling to get by since, working part time at a grocery store. Laundry Love has become an essential part of his routine, and an opportunity for a night out. "It gives me the time to come and socialize with some nice upbeat people, and feel a little bit better about myself," Clarke says.

The volunteers enjoy it, too. "I just like serving. Really, that's all it is," Ken Kawamura says. "I try to find things where people are ignored or also situations that people don't want to engage or, quote unquote, 'get their hands dirty.'"

Practicing the biblical commandment to serve your neighbor can seem daunting at times, says volunteer Shannon Kassoff—until you see the laundromat in action. "This is probably the most meaningful thing that we do, because we're taking our love outside of the walls of church," Kassoff says. "Bringing it to the people and sharing what we think is an amazing experience, and that's just love."[8]

Living in Two Kingdoms

The question that congregations need to wrestle with is, "Do we wish to participate in the reign of God?" It is a question of Christian vocation and discipleship, of living faithfully in God's world following the example of Jesus. It means taking one's faith on the road, into daily life. Mike Foss suggests that "disciples don't leave their faith in church. Disciples know no boundary between faith and life. Faith is present to intrude when temptation comes, and comfort when difficulties rise. . . . Discipleship shapes how we live."[9]

There are some Christians who think faith is a personal matter and that one should compartmentalize life into two categories that may never meet: the spiritual (matters of faith) and the temporal (life in the world). Jesus suggests it is not that simple. The Gospel of John records Jesus' prayer to his heavenly Father for his disciples then and now: "I am not asking you to take them out of the world, but I ask you to protect them from the evil one. They do not belong to the world, just as I do not belong to the world. Sanctify them in the truth; your word is truth. As you have sent me into the world, so I have sent them into the world."[10]

Luther's doctrine of the Two Kingdoms may help us understand our calling as people of faith in the world. He suggested that the Christian has two feet. One of them is planted in the spiritual realm of faith (the kingdom of God) by virtue of being a baptized child of God. The other is firmly planted in the earthly kingdom of this world. As Pastor Foss notes, today's disciples don't distinguish between a life of faith and life in this world. Disciples take a holistic approach by integrating faith and life, by living out the promises of their baptism in daily life. Disciples don't leave their faith at the church door, but take it into the world in order to make a difference for good in the lives of others. Disciples are set free from the only death that matters. In baptism one dies to sin and is made alive in Christ Jesus, now free to tell the Good News of love and salvation for all people.

The prophet Micah gives us a clue about what it means to be a church community that is faithful to God's missional calling: "What does the Lord require of you but to do justice, and to love kindness, and to walk humbly with your God?"[11] In an increasingly secular society, there is a deep spiritual hunger and an increasing moral void.

People are looking for direction, longing for purpose and meaning. Pastor Foss says that this is where *real faith meets real life.* He points out that the great desire of our time is for an authentic faith, when God's people are living their faith as real people. When today's disciples do justice, love kindness, and walk humbly with God, congregations can make an impact on their local communities and the wider world.

A Church for Others

Congregations may find that moving their ministry horizon beyond the walls of their church is not an easy task. In our book, *A Field Guide for the Missional Congregation: Embarking on a Journey of Transformation,* Craig Van Gelder and I noted that part of the problem has to do with the natural evolution of congregational life. "A major challenge facing congregations in the United States has to do with the horizon they use for framing their life and ministry. When they first come into existence, most congregations are very outreach oriented and seek to actively engage their larger community. They have the world in view as their primary horizon. Congregations that have matured, however, tend to develop complex ministries focused increasingly on the needs of their own members. Their horizon begins to turn inward toward meeting their own needs."[12]

What does it mean to be a church for others? The diagram below is an attempt to contrast a congregation with an inward focus with that of a congregation that has a more external focus. It should be understood that all congregations have elements of both types of churches. However, a missional congregation would define itself more frequently using the characteristics displayed in the righthand column.

A CHURCH FOR ME/US	A CHURCH FOR OTHERS
Focus: The local congregation	Focus: The neighborhood and the world
Valued: Membership	Valued: Discipleship
Purpose: Getting people to join	Purpose: Meeting the needs of others
Education for personal growth	Education for care and service
Worship to comfort	Worship to recharge for ministry
Small groups for nurture	Small groups for care and training
Clergy-centered	Lay-empowered
Purpose of staff: to care for members	Purpose of staff: to equip others
Pastor as primary evangelist	People as front-line missionaries
Using gifts for ministry in the church	Using gifts for ministry in daily life

This is not an exhaustive list, but it helps us identify the differences between an externally (mission) focused church and one that is internally focused. We will explore this further in the coming chapters.

We may not know exactly what the new future of God's church will look like. However, we can affirm the Spirit's action among us and seek to discern how we can participate in God's vision for mission. Perhaps the present/future look of congregations will be discipleship centers that model the early church and embrace what it means to be a church for others.

What then is God's vision for the church? It is to embrace a ministry of redemption and reconciliation for the sake of the world. St. Paul reminds us: "So if anyone is in Christ, there is a new creation: everything old has passed away; see, everything has become new! All this is from God, who reconciled the world to himself, not counting their trespasses against them, and entrusting the message of reconciliation to us [the church]."[13] The local congregation might ask how they—as the baptized people of God—are helping to fulfill God's vision of a world that is healed, redeemed, and made new.

Questions for Reflection:

1. How would you describe the *missio Dei*, God's mission plan?
2. How is the triune God a model for a relationship-centered ministry?
3. What are some ways that congregations can make visible the reign of God?
4. Do you think Luther's doctrine of the Two Kingdoms is helpful in understanding how real faith meets real life? Why or why not?
5. Which characteristics from the chart (A Church for Me/Us and A Church for Others) best describe your congregation?

Notes

1. For more of the story see Richard Rouse, *Fire of Grace: The Healing Power of Forgiveness* (Minneapolis: Augsburg Fortress, 2005).
2. Joel C. Hunter, *Church Distributed: How the Church Can Thrive in the Coming Era of Connection* (Longwood, FL: Distributed Church Press, 2007), 11.
3. Robert King, "Death and Resurrection of an Urban Church," *Faith and Leadership*, March 24, 2015. Read the entire story at www.faithandleadership.com/death-and-resurrection-urban-church.
4. Loc. cit., 16.
5. Rick Rouse and Craig Van Gelder, *A Field Guide for the Missional Congregation: Embarking on a Journey of Transformation* (Minneapolis: Augsburg Fortress, 2008), 37.
6. Luke 4:18-19 NRSV.
7. Galatians 3:28 NRSV.
8. Lisa Napoli, "A Growing Movement to Spread Faith, Love, and Clean Laundry," July 27, 2014. www.npr.org.
9. Michael W. Foss, *Reviving the Congregation: Pastoral Leadership in a Changing Context* (Minneapolis: Fortress Press, 2014), 78.
10. John 17:15-18 NRSV.
11. Micah 6:8 NRSV.

12. Rouse and Van Gelder, *A Field Guide for the Missional Congregation*, 45–46.
13. 2 Corinthians 5:18-19 NRSV.

2

From Individualism to Community: Reframing Pastoral Care

"When the Son of Man comes in his glory, and all the angels with him, then he will sit on the throne of his glory. All the nations will be gathered before him, and he will separate people one from another. . . . Then the king will say to those at his right hand, 'Come, you that are blessed by my Father, inherit the kingdom prepared for you from the foundation of the world; for I was hungry and you gave me food, I was thirsty and you gave me something to drink, I was a stranger and you welcomed me, I was naked and you gave me clothing, I was sick and you took care of me, I was in prison and you visited me. . . . Truly I tell you, just as you did it to one of the least of these brothers or sisters of mine, you did it to me.'" (Matthew 25:31–37, 40)

"I have just heard that the food banks in all of greater Des Moines are nearly empty," the pastor announced at the end of his sermon.

Then he issued the following challenge: "It is winter here in Iowa and some brothers and sisters in our community will go without food if we don't do something about it. Jesus calls us to feed the hungry, so let's get with the program. Instead of heading home to break out the snacks and cozy up for the Super Bowl, I want you to go to the nearest supermarket and fill up a *bag of groceries. There will be someone here at the church from noon until 6 p.m. this evening to receive your gift of food. Let's put our faith into action!"*

That afternoon the members of the Lutheran Church of Hope in West Des Moines, Iowa nearly cleaned out many of the grocery stores in town. Several tons of food were delivered to the church that Sunday and then distributed to the local area food banks the following day. People in the community were amazed at this outpouring of love and concern on the part of this church family. Managers of the local markets were shocked at the response and asked that they be given a "heads up" the next time!

The tradition continues to the present day. Every Super Bowl Sunday, the church hands out grocery bags to those attending worship with the expectation that the bags will return filled. In addition, the congregation takes a special offering to supplement the food items that are collected and usually raises several thousand dollars. It is but one of many ways that this congregation expresses its care and concern for their community.

The words of Jesus in the Gospel of Matthew call us to a greater purpose outside of ourselves and beyond the walls of our churches. Just as we have been loved by God, so we are to show love and care for the lonely, the outcast, the hungry, the homeless, and others in need.

Changing the Paradigm

"The worship has ended, let the service begin" is a sign that adorns the exit doors of many churches. It is a reminder that the people of God gather not only to be spiritually fed by word and sacrament, but that this is only a means to an end: Christians are nurtured and strengthened so they may better serve God and others in daily life. Some congregations express it another way: "Gathered to Scatter" suggests that the faithful *come together* for the purpose of *going out* again with a renewed sense of passion to share the love of God in word and deed in order to bring healing to the world around them.

Bethany Lutheran Church is a congregation in the Greater Denver area that decided to cancel their regular Sunday worship schedule on the first Sunday in May. Members were encouraged to spend an hour or more that same weekend engaged in some service project. Various community agencies were contacted in advance so that people would have a variety of options to choose from. The reader board in front of the church announced: "This Sunday we are worshiping by serving our sisters and brothers in the community." One communion service was made available on Sunday morning, while over a thousand people of all ages made an impact by their service that weekend. Photos of the congregation in action were posted on the church website and Facebook page. And a number of these servants found the experience so rewarding that they have continued to be involved in particular acts of care.

The above illustrations of congregations who have chosen to focus on the needs of those in the larger community around them is a sign of the church returning to its roots of care (Acts 2:44-47) and reclaiming God's mission of healing and redemption as seen in the last chapter. But it is much more than a renewed and more vigorous form of outreach ministry being practiced by a growing number of congregations. It represents an important shift in how one understands pastoral care. It can also be symptomatic of a cultural shift in congregations—from a preoccupation with care for those inside the church, often centered on the individual—to a greater sense of community care and a concern for the common good.

This is a paradigm shift, if you will, from the *traditional* view of pastoral care where a pastor, trained professional, or lay caregiver devotes their time and energy to meeting the needs of an individual or family connected with a given institution. This includes pastors providing marriage counseling, Stephen Ministers (trained lay caregivers) visiting the homebound, spiritual directors guiding their directees in listening for God's Spirit, hospital chaplains ministering to patients and their families, mental health counselors offering assistance to those with acute problems, and the like. All of these are examples of important, caring ministry.

There is a great deal of literature that was written in the 1960s and 70s about the primary role of the pastor being that of an *in-house counselor*. Seminary students preparing to be parish pastors were taught the principles of good counseling and reminded of important guidelines when ministering to members of their congregation. Among the rules they were expected to follow included the following: 1) Don't try to solve a person's problem for them, but guide them to finding a solution for themselves; 2) Do not allow yourself to get romantically or sexually involved; 3) Set realistic expectations and boundaries such as how much time and when you are available; and 4) Be aware when you have exceeded your expertise and need to refer them to another professional who can better assist them.

I recall a couple of incidents from my time as a college chaplain where I was able to draw on my seminary training in counseling. The first involved a young co-ed who had just returned to campus following her brother's funeral. She asked to meet me in my office that Sunday evening as she was very distraught. She proceeded to tell me that her brother had committed suicide the previous week. And at the funeral, the pastor told the family he was sorry that the young boy would likely not go to heaven because of the action of taking his own life. The second incident took place the day before graduation. I was asked by the college administration to go in person to the room of the young man who had been captain of the football team. I needed to let him know that his father had died that morning of a heart attack and would not be attending his son's graduation the next day. I was indeed grateful for the practical and biblical resources I was able to call on to assist these college students in their time of need.

Effective counseling and caregiving are and continue to be important ways of sharing God's love with those in need. In fact, there are times in our lives when we can and should avail ourselves of the services of a professional counselor, coach, or trained spiritual director. People need help dealing with grief, addiction, family conflict, vocational direction, and other challenges that life throws at them. Family or Group Counseling can also be helpful when dealing with common issues and where the sharing of stories can benefit all. Alcoholics Anonymous, Survivors of Divorce, and grief groups led by trained facilitators are all good examples of this.

The Challenge of Pastoral Care

A problem arises when we limit ourselves to a traditional understanding of pastoral care. The challenge can be manifested in several ways. In smaller congregations that are often called "Pastoral Size Congregations"—with seventy-five or fewer worshipers per week—there is the expectation that the pastor knows and cares about everyone in his or her flock. There is a high bar to be met by anyone who comes to provide public ministry in this setting. The pastor should know everyone by name and even be aware when there is someone in need. Often it is assumed that the pastor will come to visit one in the hospital even if the pastor or church office has not been notified. People expect personal attention from their pastor and can be resentful if someone other than the pastor seeks to attend to their needs. Some come to have a myopic view of the church, believing it exists solely for their own benefit and the benefit of others in their church family. There can be resentment when the pastor spends time involved with community projects or suggests that members of the congregation likewise have a responsibility for those outside their church walls.

Pastoral caregivers themselves can be part of the problem. Some pastors who willingly identify themselves as the counselor-in-residence may tend to neglect other necessary pastoral duties. They may feel content to "put out their shingle" and advertise that they are available most days at certain hours to hear anyone and everyone's problems and concerns. Or they may pride themselves in never being in the office, because they are always calling on parishioners. They are out doing the Lord's work by visiting the homebound, the sick in the hospital, people who are new to the community, or those who have fallen away from the church. All of these pastoral acts have good intentions behind them. Pastors who recognize the importance of balance in their ministry see that pastoral care is but one of many tasks that require their attention. And they would do well to remind their members of the same.

Carey Nieuwhof, Pastor of Connexus Church near Toronto and author of *Leading Change without Losing It*, suggests that a traditional view of pastoral care can actually hinder the vitality and growth of most churches. He believes that this very issue can be detrimental to health of every church and pastor. He writes in his blog, "How Pastoral Care Stunts the Growth of Most Churches":

> When the pastor has to visit every sick person, do every wedding and funeral and make regular house calls, attend every meeting, and lead every bible study or group, he or she becomes incapable of doing almost anything else. Message preparation falls to the side, and providing organizational leadership for the future is almost out of the question. The pastoral care model of church leadership simply doesn't scale. It's somewhat ironic, actually. If you're a good pastoral care person (and many pastors are), people will often love you so much that the church will grow to two hundred people, at which point the pastoral care expectations become crushing. Inevitably, pastoral leaders with larger churches can't keep up and end up disappointing people when they

can't get to every event any more. Caring for thirty people personally is possible. Caring for two hundred and thirty is not. Many pastors burn out trying.

The pastoral care model most seminaries teach and most congregations embrace creates false and unsustainable expectations. Consequently, almost everyone gets hurt in the process. The pastor is frustrated that he or she can't keep up. And the congregation is frustrated over the same thing. Eventually the pastor burns out or leaves, and the church shrinks back to a smaller number. If a new pastor arrives who also happens to be good at pastoral care, the pattern simply repeats itself; growth, frustration, burnout, exit . . .

If a church is going to grow, congregations have to let go of the expectation that their pastor will be available for every medical emergency, every twist and turn in their lives, every family celebration and every crisis. That's a tough sell for many congregations, but if a church is going to grow, it has to happen. So how do you deal with this? Have the courage to shift care to the congregation. . . . I'm convinced that if we change how we do pastoral care, we'd reach more people. And in the process, we'd care for people much better than we do now.[1]

Pastors and other caregivers can also oversimplify an issue or solution when ministering to a person in need. Some pastoral caregivers will quickly assume that prayer can solve the problem without understanding the context or complexity of a given situation. It can be easy to jump to a conclusion or be so eager to get to a solution that one misses the deeper pain or burden being carried by an individual. Carrie Doehring, in her book *The Practice of Pastoral Care: A Postmodern Approach*, suggests that we view our ministry of care through the trifocal lenses of a premodern, modern, and postmodern approach to counseling:

Using a *premodern* lens, pastors assume for the moment that God or that which is sacred can be glimpsed and apprehended to some degree through sacred texts, religious rituals and traditions, and religious and spiritual experiences—the way transcendent realities seemed to be known with the ancient and medieval church prior. . . . Using a *modern* lens, pastoral caregivers draw upon rational and empirical methods, like biblical critical methods, medical knowledge, and the social sciences, in offering pastoral care. A *postmodern* lens brings into focus the contextual and provisional nature of knowledge, including knowledge of God.[2]

Rethinking Pastoral Care as Community Care

Do the needs of the individual outweigh the needs of the many? That is a question that is not asked enough in our American culture of individualism. It seems we have become so preoccupied with championing the rights of the individual, that we often overlook what needs to be done for the "common good." This is true in all of our institutions including the local congregation. Pastoral care need not be limited to individuals within church walls. Our understanding of pastoral care can be expanded to include all our sisters and brothers who are outside the walls of the congregation. This way of thinking moves us beyond a traditional approach to pastoral care—as important as it is—to recognizing that God's care is not just personal but is intended for the entire community.

Rick Barger suggests "having a personal relationship with Jesus in the presumed manner that pervades our culture today is not a prevalent theme in the New Testament. . . . Whatever references there are to personal issues of faith in the New Testament, they are always within the context of the work of Jesus' gathering of the church. Almost all of what Jesus has to say in the New Testament comes at the church in the plural form of the word *you*."[3]

A new way of thinking about pastoral care in our postmodern, post-Christian culture might be called *community care*. It does not take away anything from the importance of caring for the individual in need. Rather it expands our understanding of the nature and purpose of pastoral care that coincides with God's vision for the church as a community of care for all. "The emphasis on community is not to belittle the individual or to mean that the individual is not important.

The lifting up of the value and primacy of the community actually serves to elevate the value of the individual."[4]

The congregation is not just a group of individuals who have gathered out of a common need. It is a community of God's people who are called to a common purpose: sharing the gospel of Jesus' love with a world in need. Called by God in baptism, Christians bind themselves to one another and to God in a cause greater than themselves. St. Peter writes (using the plural form of you): "You are a chosen race, a royal priesthood, a holy nation, God's own people, in order that you may proclaim the mighty acts of him who called you out of darkness into his marvelous light. Once you were not a people, but now you are God's people; once you had not received mercy, but now you have received mercy."[5]

The emphasis on community care is not to suggest that congregations simply expand their social concerns or outreach programs, but is rather intended to instill a "new" way of understanding the very nature of the church. The church as a congregation was never intended to be an end in itself, but rather a means to an end. When Jesus said "follow me" he suggested that the church embrace God's mission of extending mercy and hope to all people. The church was to be God's partner in ushering in the *reign of God* that had become incarnate in Jesus Christ. The very character of Jesus was to be a model for the church. It was to make manifest the gifts of peace, justice, grace, hope, and love in and for all of creation.

Releasing the Gifts of God's People

The new paradigm of pastoral care is intended to unleash the gifts of all God's people for ministry in daily life. *Community Care* is a way of expanding our understanding that pastoral care is not just about the pastor or a few trained individuals offering care for church members and their families. It is about reclaiming the New Testament notion that the gifts of God's people are intended for the healing of the whole community, not just those in the church. It is a movement from individual care to communal care. This suggests that the Christian is not to be content with simply receiving care and nurture in the faith, but is called to live out one's faith by caring for others.

The old paradigm of church hierarchy is best illustrated with a traditional pyramid that showed the clergy on top and members of the congregation on the bottom. This could signify two things: one, that the pastor was the primary evangelist who shared God's Word, and two, that the pastor was the servant of all, with members of the congregation the recipients of the care and ministry provided by the pastor, staff, and church leaders. In the new paradigm, members of the congregation are seen as the front-line missionaries and caregivers serving others in the larger community in the name of Jesus. The ideal of how a congregation lives out its God-given purpose is illustrated by an *Inverted Pyramid*, which suggests the equipping of the saints comes from the bottom up and shows how God's people are supported for their work in the world.

The Inverted Pyramid

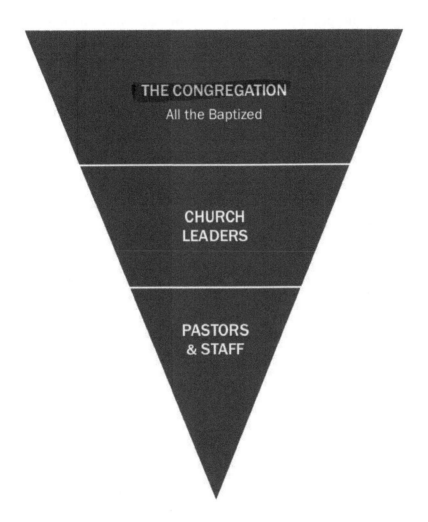

I became acutely aware of this new paradigm when I was installed as pastor in my first congregation. The bishop preached that morning and his admonishment to the congregation was this: "If your pastor is doing anything that you as members could be doing then you have failed in your role to be a functioning Body of Christ in mission."

The focus on releasing the gifts of God's people in the world requires the church to recognize that its primary ministry is *equipping disciples to live their baptismal faith in service to others*. To do so, we recapture the idea that the role of the pastor and others in professional ministry is to enable God's people to do their ministry in the world. In Ephesians we read: "The gifts [God] gave were that some would be apostles, some prophets, some evangelists, some pastors and teachers, *to equip the saints for the work of ministry*, for the building up the body of Christ."[6] In other words, pastors and other trained leaders have a clearly defined role: to empower all of God's people to use their gifts and passion for their everyday ministry.

Rather than church members seeing themselves simply as customers of care, those in the larger community who are served by congregational members become the customer. Rather than insisting that every ministry revolves in and around the church building, a new paradigm or missional congregation seeks to reorient its ministry toward the neighborhood by building bridges to those beyond the walls of the church. "This reversal of emphasis is nothing less than the Copernican revolution of the church. It is a reorientation; it is becoming the church that centers and revolves around others rather than insisting on believing 'our church' is the center of the universe."[7]

The New Face of Community Care

We find ourselves living in a complex society. Incredible cultural shifts have occurred over the past fifty years as the United States has seen a growing diversity in ethnicity, religious beliefs, sexual norms, generational differences, a growing divide between the rich and poor, and increased political polarity. It is not easy figuring out how to be the church in a post-Christian, postmodern world that offers so many challenges and no simple solutions.

Congregations may yearn for days long past when it was assumed that churches and their communities were more homogeneous in ethnicity and religious belief. It is debated whether the United States was ever a Christian nation, but recent studies as mentioned in the Introduction suggest that we are now a very diverse, multifaith population. And racism continues to haunt our country with cries for justice and equality taking the form of many voices, from Latino, to Asian, to African American.

Even as this book is being written, the cry of "Black Lives Matter" is being heard throughout cities around the country in response to perceived racial profiling and police brutality that has resulted in the deaths of African American men and boys. There is also concern about the alarming rise of extremist groups espousing the ideals of "white supremacy" that view all races other than Caucasian with suspicion and distain.

The historic Emanuel AME church in Charleston was shaken to its core when a young white male, age twenty-one, gunned down nine parishoners after joining them for a midweek Bible study. As the incident was being investigated as a hate crime and blatant act of racism, realtives of the victims described their pain and anger but also spoke of love. They forgave the accused, inviting him to repent and receive God's mercy. Religious leaders in the greater Charleston area came together in a show of unity and support, saying they would not be defined by hate. An act that was intended to divide them became a rallying cry for solidarity.

In the aftermath of the Charleston tragedy, the Lutheran bishop of South Carolina, Herman Yoos, invited the congregations in his synod to join in a new conversation about race. In doing so, he cited a book, *The Church Enslaved: A Spirituality of Racial Reconciliation*, by

Tony Campollo and Michael Battle in which the authors suggest that the 11:00 hour on Sunday morning is still the most segregated hour in America. They identify five behaviors of white Americans that contribute to this climate: "patronization of whites toward blacks, blaming the victim, avoiding social contact, denying cultural differences, and denying the political significance of these differences."[8]

It is into this world that God calls the church to a mission of healing and reconciliation. This is not an easy task, nor is it an easy time to be the church for the sake of the world. A biracial clergy couple was called to serve in a redevelopment ministry in Baltimore. They were tasked with bringing together two small, primarily white congregations that were struggling. One had twenty-five in worship and the other nineteen on any given Sunday. Eventually one building was sold and they begin worshiping together in one church facility. This, of course, did not solve the problem of viability and vitality for mission. The pastors challenged them to reach out and be more welcoming of others, especially their neighbors of other ethnic backgrounds. A large banner was hung near the front door of the church that read "Everyone welcome. No exceptions." Upon which one of the members asked the pastor: "When do we get to vote on that sign?" The pastor's reply was, "This is not a matter we vote on."

Jesus has called his church to open the door wide for everyone to come in and receive God's gift of grace that brings healing, forgiveness, and life. Likewise, the church is invited to go out and share those gifts freely with those in the community regardless of race, creed, gender, or economic status. Both the Old and New Testament admonish the people of God to reach out to all people, especially those on the margins, and take a stand for justice, peace, and equality.

Being Open to People of Different Faith Traditions

The Christian church is invited to work closely with people of other faiths to bring about God's vision of justice, peace, and equality for all people. As the world faces various crises such as poverty, hunger, war, human trafficking, child and spousal abuse, disease, lack of access to clean water, and so on, it is imperative that people of faith come together to find common solutions. It can be overwhelming for any one congregation. And in chapter six, we will explore the idea of forming community partnerships to address local issues.

One of the challenges of establishing relationships with persons or organizations of different faith traditions is the "us/them" barrier. People of one faith may have a prejudiced point of view and misconceptions about those whose faith is different from their own. There may be an unfounded fear that those who are not like us may pose a threat to our own religious beliefs. Whether it be a matter of ethnic or faith diversity in our communities, bigotry often raises its ugly head and keeps neighbors apart. In their book *Leading Diverse Communities: A How-To Guide for Moving from Healing into Action*, Cherie Brown and George Mazza suggest that the key to understanding and building of relationships lies in sharing one another's stories:

> Many of us have gone to great lengths to change someone's bigoted attitude. We have tried to convince them by pointing out the errors of their position. We have tried to give them new information. In the end we have walked away frustrated, certain that people will just never change. New information rarely changes people, but hearing personal stories of discrimination can transform the most hardened hearts. We can refute facts and figures, but we can't refute someone's story. Authentic stories of the heart have their own reasons that can be more persuasive than the most carefully crafted arguments. We don't change people's minds, we change their hearts.[9]

Pastor Jane Buckley-Farlee is Pastor of Trinity Lutheran Congregation in the Cedar Riverside neighborhood of Minneapolis. It has always been a "first stop" for immigrants, beginning with Scandinavians in the past. Today many of Trinity's immigrant neighbors are Somali and of the Muslim faith. Jane shared her interfaith story of how her Lutheran congregation has found ways to work with and deepen relationships with today's immigrant community. The neighborhood mosque had been severely damaged by fire. The day of the fire she went to the scene to be a supportive presence and subsequently attended several neighborhood meetings. Trinity's council did not hesitate a second to reach out to their Muslim sisters and brothers; Trinity congregation opened its doors to them while they rebuilt their mosque.

Fledgling relationships of mutual trust and respect were greatly deepened through the engagement of the two communities of faith. And when the mosque was remodeled, the front door of the worship center faced the neighborhood—unlike a more traditional structure—as a sign of a greater sense of partnership with and openness to the community. And likewise, it is not unusual for the Trinity church electronic sign to wish people a "Blessed Ramadan."

Pastor Buckley-Farlee cautions that building bridges between different faith traditions is not easy. She says it is really slow, really hard, and wonderful. It calls for letting go of how we think things should work out. One ends up changed in ways one didn't plan on or maybe didn't want. It happens when people are willing to invest in relationships that are mutually sincere.

Fortunately there is a growing awareness that many in the multifaith community most of us live in have a similar hope and goal of bringing God's healing care to others. One example of this is how leaders and people of many faiths came together in prayer after the tragedy of 9/11. Some congregations are engaged in interfaith dialogue at the local level; religious leaders meet to discuss their similarities and differences, while inviting their colleagues to lead forums that describe their religious tradition. When I was a pastor in Phoenix, I invited both a Jewish rabbi and an imam (Muslim cleric) to talk to members of my congregation. We discovered more about their faith traditions, including the fact that our respective religions had a common origin in the Old Testament figure of Abraham.

It is encouraging that barriers between Christian denominations are breaking down as ecumenical conversations continue to explore the common mission of care that churches of different traditions share. While differences and divisions still exist in the universal Christian church, many are finding ways to work together locally and around the world to share the gospel of God's love in tangible ways. Habitat for Humanity has been one of a number of causes that have brought people from different faith backgrounds together in an effort to build affordable housing. Hunger appeals such as Feed My Starving Children have allowed those from both sacred and secular worlds to find common ground and a way of helping others together. There will still be those in a variety of faith traditions that will choose to "go it alone" for reasons such as maintaining purity of doctrine and a concern about diluting their values by working or worshiping with those unlike themselves. However, it is encouraging that pan-Christian and interfaith cooperation seems to be on the rise.

Living Faithfully in God's World

Every congregation might ask itself if it is a welcoming place where everyone is welcome—no exceptions. Every congregation might ask itself if it knows and cares for the neighbor, those outside the church walls. These two questions go hand-in-hand as God's people seek to live faithfully in God's world. Adopting the new paradigm of *community care* as a common mission for the congregation may provide a way forward. As we will see in the chapters ahead, this new understanding of pastoral care can become an opportunity for congregations to participate in the reign of God ushered in and made incarnate by Jesus.

We are talking about a church turned inside out and upside down. This is a church that cares for and nurtures it members for the purpose of creating and empowering new disciples for missionary work in the world. This church equips people according to their gifts to serve others (1 Cor. 12:7). This is a church that reaches beyond church walls in an effort to build relationships and partnerships with those who may be different from themselves. A new paradigm congregation is "a church that values and makes the most of differences in the Body of Christ and works through outside relationships not just inside programs. . . . Linking differences and bridging distances for the benefit of all is a key element."[10]

Congregations are called to be a welcoming place for all people, one that follows the example of Jesus and the early church. Jesus welcomed the outcast, the sinner, and those in disrepute to come to him and be ministered to. Can the church of today do any less? The following hymn by Marty Haugen serves as both a challenge and an opportunity for the local congregation:

> Let us build a house where hands will reach beyond the wood and stone
> To heal and strengthen, serve and teach, and love the Word they've known.
> Here the outcast and the stranger bear the image of God's face;
> Let us bring an end to fear and danger. . . .
> Let us build a house where all are named, their songs and visions heard
> And loved and treasured, taught and claimed as words within the Word.
> Built of tears and cries of laughter, prayers of faith and songs of grace,
> Let this house proclaim from floor to rafter: All are welcome,
> All are welcome, all are welcome in this place.[11]

Questions for Reflection:

1. What are some examples of the traditional view of pastoral care? What are the benefits to this approach? What are the drawbacks or constraints to this understanding of care?
2. How would you describe the "new" paradigm of pastoral care that the author refers to as community care?
3. Why do some congregations find it hard to move from a traditional model of pastoral care (focused on their own care) to a biblical, missional model of care for others?
4. What are some of the challenges of partnering in ministry with people of different denominations and different faith traditions? How might they be addressed?
5. Do you believe that your congregation is a welcoming place for all people? Why or why not?

Notes

1. Carey Nieuwhof, "How Pastoral Care Stunts the Growth of Most Churches." See full blogpost at: http://careynieuwhof.com/2015/11/how-pastoral-care-stunts-the-growth-of-most-churches/.
2. Carrie Doehring, *The Practice of Pastoral Care: A Postmodern Approach* (Louisville: Westminster John Knox, 2006), 2.
3. Rick Barger, *A New and Right Spirit: Creating an Authentic Church in a Consumer Culture* (Herndon, VA: Alban Institute, 2005), 86.
4. Ibid., 88.
5. 1 Peter 2:9-10.
6. Ephesians 4:11-12.
7. Joel C. Hunter, *Church Distributed: How the Church Can Thrive in the Coming Era of Connection* (Longwood, FL: Distributed Church Press, 2007), 147–48.
8. From an article by ELCA Bishop Herman Yoos, "A New Conversation About Race," quoting from the book by Tony Campollo and Michael Battle, *The Church Enslaved: A Spirituality of Racial Reconciliation*. South Carolina

Synod E-Newsletter distributed June 22, 2015, http://archive.constant contact.com/fs164/1102200742508/archive/1120881406225.html.

9. Cherie R. Brown and George J. Mazza, *Leading Diverse Communities: A How-To Guide for Moving from Healing into Action* (San Francisco: Jossey-Bass, 2005), 97.

10. Hunter, *Church Distributed*, 16–17.

11. Marty Haugen, "All Are Welcome," Evangelical Lutheran Worship (Minneapolis: Augsburg Fortress, 2006), hymn 641. Text and music ©1994 GIA Publications, Inc.

3

Maneuvering the Challenges of Change

Do not be conformed to this world, but be transformed [changed] by the renewing of your minds, so that you may discern what is the will of God—what is good, and acceptable, and perfect. (Romans 12:2)

Sanctuary is a blended congregation of the ELCA and United Methodist Church located in Marshfield, Massachusetts. It is a congregation that recognizes the changes going on in its community as well as changes in how one understands church today. The congregation likes to think outside the box, and their mission statement is simple: "Create. Connect. Respond."

> *Sanctuary, a 4-year old congregation, has a new way of doing church. . . . Worship doesn't necessarily follow the lectionary but takes an educational approach, said its pastor, Mark Huber, who will often explain one parable over multiple weeks. "Our one constant is change, so we're always trying to look for a new way to connect and be creative," he said. . . . "The church's style is about seeing God at work in the world in new ways. . . . God has always been faithful to the church and the church is always being made new. We strive to be faithful to a God who is calling us to do this. We help people see how the gospel is playing out in their lives."[1]*

Congregations must be open to change and the moving of God's

Spirit if they are to live into the future God has called them to embrace. Just as the early disciples of Jesus discovered, there will be many surprises along the way and change is inevitable. Church leaders would do well to foster a spirit of imagination, encouraging people to dream about new possibilities.

Gary Nelson, in his book *Borderland Churches: A Congregation's Introduction to Missional Living*, talks about congregations like Sanctuary that live in that sweet spot between the world of faith and the world of culture, seeking to bridge the gap between these two worlds. He calls them "borderland churches." And he goes on to say that "imagination allows the borderland to be a place of adventure and transformation. It flows from the ability of people living in the borderland to hope and to place their fears aside. . . . Imagination is the wide-eyed wonder that people and circumstances can change, that things do not have to remain the same."[2]

Dealing with Change

Change, as they say, is inevitable. However, change can be difficult, especially for established institutions like the church. It is not easy, for example, for many congregations to make the shift from a maintenance-oriented and membership-dominated ministry to a missional and discipleship culture. This chapter will attempt to provide a pathway to healthy change in congregations. We will first explore different reactions to change and some of the causes of resistance to change. We will consider the importance of congregational climate change as a prelude to changing the DNA of the congregation. Finally, we will reflect on the difference between technical and adaptive solutions in response to change.

A congregation like any human institution will find that members react to change in a variety of ways. As we see in the diagram below, some readily embrace it while others dig in their heels and resist it. Others are simply resigned to the fact that change is inevitable.

Different Responses to Change[3]

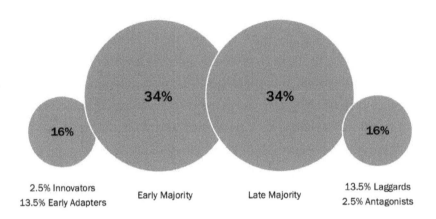

| 2.5% Innovators | Early Majority | Late Majority | 13.5% Laggards |
| 13.5% Early Adapters | | | 2.5% Antagonists |

This is a sociological model that demonstrates a broad range of responses to change. There are usually about 16 percent of the members of an organization that wish to lead the charge for change. This group is made up of 2.5 percent who are innovators, suggesting and offering a plan for change, as well as 13.5 percent who are early adapters and cheerleaders for change. What follows are the early majority and late majority, making up 34 percent each. These are the people who, once convinced that a particular action and subsequent change is necessary and important, willingly get on board—some sooner, some later. The last 16 percent consist of those who are often threatened by any kind of change and try to hang on to the status quo. Thirteen and a half percent of this last group drag their feet in resistance; while 2.5 percent can be downright hostile and may choose to fight change to the bitter end.

The problem with many organizations is one of *homeostasis*. This is the tendency of an institution or congregation to prefer the status quo, wishing to stay the same. Changes may be suggested and even put in place, but resistance often results in abandoning new initiatives in order to return to what has been. Congregations, for example, can allow a small minority to derail a proposed program or action because they are intimidated by those resisting change. This often results in the loss of those in the leading 16 percent who become frustrated with the lack of progress. Healthy institutions are those that value innovation and understand that change is inevitable. They take seriously the first 16 percent who can lead the organization or congregation forward into a more vital and dynamic future. While not ignoring the resisters, they don't allow the "tail to wag the dog," while offering them care and understanding.

Changing the Climate

Assessing the climate in order to change the culture is the first step. Church leaders should ask how healthy is the family system of the congregation. Are people open and trusting with one another, or is there suspicion and a tendency to blame others without having all the information? Are members open to change and new opportunities, or are they closed-minded, preferring to live in the past? What would it take to cultivate a healthier climate in the congregation that would help people be more open to change and innovation? Only then can the leadership begin to consider a cultural shift to becoming a more discipleship-centered and mission-oriented congregation.

One of the major tasks for leaders of change is to manage the anxiety level of members in a congregation. The comment that it is "change that makes us uncomfortable" is a widely accepted half-truth, according to Robert Kegan and Lisa Lahey. In their book *Immunity to Change: How to Overcome It and Unlock the Potential in Yourself and Your Organization*, they suggest that it is not simply change itself that causes anxiety in the system. Rather "it is change that leaves us feeling defenseless before the dangers we 'know' to be present that causes us anxiety."[4] Some people may feel that the rug is being taken out from underneath them when it comes to change. They may feel defenseless or powerless in the advent of change.

Leaders can deal with anxiety in the system by offering a non-anxious or low-anxious presence. It is important to stay calm and not be caught up in the emotions of the moment, genuinely listening to the concerns expressed while offering reassurance that God will lead the congregation safely forward. At the same time, it is important that congregational leaders not get too far ahead of the congregation in their suggestions for change. Successful church leaders will seek to build ownership for a new vision. One of the ways to do this and also to minimize anxiety is to communicate three things to members of a congregation: 1) what will *not* change, 2) what *will* change and why, and 3) how the changes will help the congregation move forward as faithful partners in God's larger mission vision.

It is important to let people know that the leadership is not proposing to "throw the baby out with the bathwater" but rather to maintain those things the congregation deeply cares about while at the same time seeking change. The question is not just about what must we give up in order to have a vital future, but also what values and elements of our ministry should be preserved and strengthened? What are the good things of today that the congregation can build on moving forward? When assisting one of my congregations adopt a more flexible governing structure to better facilitate ministry in our community, I indicated that as a Lutheran congregation we would continue to center our lives around the Word and Sacraments. When this was clearly stated, some of the anxiety went away. Successful transformation takes the best from a congregation's traditions, identity, and history into its future.

Another strategy for helping people deal with change is to offer them options. "As people experience the emergence of options where before there were none, they begin to feel new energy and hope. . . . New ways of thinking permit new ways of feeling, and new ways of feeling encourage and validate new ways of thinking. Energy that had been trapped in the [organization's] immune system is now released."[5] An example of this comes from a congregation that was involved in a building program. When the time came to decide what kind of seating to have in the Worship Center, the Building Committee offered a number of choices with people speaking to the advantages of each of them. Successful change comes from an increased sense of control and participation.

Church leaders who wish to initiate cultural change to sustain a new vision for mission will cultivate trust in their leadership and the process of change. They will seek to lower the anxiety level by managing their own anxiety. They will attempt manageable levels of change. In some cases, it is enough to suggest that the congregation is experimenting with something new, and if it doesn't succeed that is okay too. They can learn from the experience and move on to the next thing they feel God's Spirit is leading them to do or try. Above all, building and maintaining trust is crucial for transforming the climate and initiating a culture of innovation.

Altering the Congregation's DNA

The goal of cultural transformation for the sake of mission involves changing the DNA of a congregation. This happens as a congregation lives into its new future by cultivating a core identity that connects with their present context. In his book *Missional Map-*

Making: Skills for Leading in Times of Transition, Alan Roxburgh discusses the challenge facing most congregations in dealing with the dramatic changes in the culture:

> The change in the environment in which our churches are located has been dramatic. A first step in missional planning involves taking the time to become aware of this incredible change in our own contexts. Our tendency as leaders is to rely mostly on such tools as demographic data or internal assessments about how people in the church feel about certain programs (worship, youth, evangelism, and so on) but not attend to these environmental changes. Without attending to these transformations in our environment, we will miss what is happening in our world, and our planning will continue to reach Christians from other churches rather than the people in this new world.[6]

Congregations that are serious about embracing God's mission future understand that they can no longer cling with nostalgia to the past. The temptation for many is to seek to return to the mid-twentieth century when worship centers and Sunday school buildings were full. Doing and being church seemed easier then. Congregations would do well to fast-forward to the future and contemplate the challenges of being church in the twenty-first century. They can ask themselves what must change in our DNA—how we understand what it means to be church—if they are to be faithful to where God is calling them to serve their neighbors in this day and age. Consider the following story of a new congregation that decided to "do church" in a different way.

The members of Arlington Presbyterian Church discovered that the church was more than just a building. It was people. When they realized that the people who worked and shopped in the neighborhood surrounding the church couldn't afford to live there, they chose to do something radical. They have decided to tear down their church facility so that affordable housing can be built in its place; then they'll rent ground-floor space in the building so members can continue to worship on the same site where they have been for the past one hundred years.

The church members asked themselves, "For whom are our hearts breaking?" They set out to find the answer by quizzing the waitresses, teachers and store clerks who bought from the food truck in the church parking lot or shopped at the nearby farmers market in Arlington's fast-gentrifying Columbia Pike neighborhood. Again and again, they heard the same worries from working-class residents, many of them immigrants: "I work here, but I can't afford to live here anymore."

The century-old congregation decided to sell its building, parking lot and grounds to the Arlington Partnership for Affordable Housing, which will tear down the stone structure and replace it with 173 affordable apartments...The church's goals are twofold: to ensure their own financial viability while easing a growing crisis for low-earning people in a region where the cost of housing keeps going up...

Arlington Presbyterian Church members have understood the problem intellectually for years. But it wasn't until they began speaking to their neighbors that the crisis made an emotional impact. Elder Susan Etherton, one of seven members who did the outreach, said when the group reported back to the congregation, she could almost see people's perspectives shift. "When they heard those stories of heartbreak, there was head-nodding and agreement," she said. "When you tell personal stories, they have a resonance."[7]

The leadership of the congregation in Arlington, Virginia started a visioning process by getting to know their community context. The congregation wanted to reach out with the gospel of God's love and decided the best way was by trying to meet the felt needs of people around them. They didn't want a church building for themselves but one that would serve their community. They listened to God's Spirit and the voices of people in their neighborhood. They were open to change and imagined doing ministry in a new way in a changing neighborhood. Now after conversations with city and community leaders, they are excited about how their property will now be able to serve the needs of the community around them.

Taking the Temperature

Church leaders may wish to "take the temperature" of the congregation as they seek to open the congregation to further change and transformation. It involves taking an inventory of values, attitudes, and challenges. There are many instruments available that can offer a helpful assessment of where members see themselves and the church, as well as the direction they'd like to go. Below is a simple exercise that can be used with focus groups in the congregation.

Who We Are and What We Hope to Become

1. Make a list of core values that you think the congregation lives by.
2. Which of these core values are especially important if the congregation is to be faithful to where God is calling us to serve the gospel in today's world?
3. How would you describe the health of the congregation? 1 is low, 5 is high.
4. Trust in leadership   1 2 3 4 5
5. Financial viability and transparency 1 2 3 4 5
6. Respectful of each other   1 2 3 4 5
7. Clear sense of purpose and mission 1 2 3 4 5
8. Spiritual growth (e.g., worship life)   1 2 3 4 5
9. If the congregation ceased to exist, would the community miss it? Why or why not?
10. What needs to change (e.g., attitudes, resources, etc.) if the congregation is to move forward into God's promised, missional future?

For any transformation process to be successful, a congregation must choose to change. It must be willing to alter the DNA of the congregation so that it is more confident and open to the future God is calling it to embrace. "The only recipe for healthy growth is intentional, committed, and consistent change. That is true at the personal level as well as on the organizational plane. . . . Effective leaders of change will bring others on board and have a team that supports one another in the stresses of leading change in the congregation."[8]

The following story is one example of a smaller congregation that questioned its viability until their pastor suggested they do an inventory of their assets and see how this might lead to a change in how they viewed themselves and their potential for sustaining a viable ministry in their community. It all happened when Pastor Bev Piro arrived at St. Andrew Lutheran Church in Arvada, Colorado.

They were asking themselves, "Are we going to be able to continue?" With only fifty people in worship each Sunday, the congregation was "wallowing in grief" about their smaller size and not being able to do ministry as they once could, such as sustain a Sunday school.

Last summer, Piro helped the congregation launch a discernment process, taking stock of their strengths and assets. Through this process, members noted that their building, fully paid off, was an underused asset. Without a viable Sunday school, the eight-room education wing was being used only for storage.

But an inefficient use of space wasn't the heart of the problem, Piro said. Without any purpose, these rooms served as a visible "reminder of who they had been," she added. "It was abandoned and it felt awful."

Through a serendipitous conversation with a member, Piro and the congregational council began to research the possibility of renting space to a mental health counseling office and then to a massage therapist. Council members had to work through their concerns about the impact of charging rent on the congregation's tax-exempt status, but legal advice helped them understand how to make it work.

In October 2014, on the day the Christian church honors physician/evangelist Luke, the "St. Andrew Lutheran Church Healing Arts Center" was dedicated.

"It's been remarkable," said Piro, noting a change in the congregation's spirit and vitality.

The congregation used to lock the sanctuary during the day, but now the doors are always open, inviting guests inside. A healing arts fair introduced visitors to the building, strengthening the congregation's community presence. The tenants are also doing well, with one business expanding into a second office space at the church.

The congregation's renewed focus has made a difference. There's a "really good spirit here now and people are noticing"—and visitors are starting to show up at worship, Piro said. Congregational growth, however, was never the point, she said. St. Andrew now has a presence and role in the community. "[Members] are seeing themselves as . . .

a hub of activity that extends outside of Sunday morning. . . . It's like we're walking out of the catacombs of death into life," Piro said.[9]

Adaptive Leaders Seek Adaptive Solutions

It is helpful to distinguish between two kinds of change challenges that Ron Heifetz of the Harvard Business School calls "technical" and "adaptive." Church leaders who seek to promote a climate of care and implement effective solutions to congregational and community issues understand that different circumstances call for different approaches to change.

People are often too eager to apply technical or timeworn solutions to problems that may require creative thinking and a new adaptive approach. The challenges a congregation faces today and tomorrow may require something more than merely using a technical approach to solve a problem when adaptive challenges require a new mindset and a creative approach. "We may be unable to bring about the changes we want because we are misdiagnosing our aspiration as technical, when in reality it is an adaptive challenge. The implication is that we must find adaptive (nontechnical) means of supporting ourselves and others to meet adaptive challenges."[10]

Technical problems such as open-heart surgery can be approached in a technical manner. One uses current knowledge and skills to apply a known solution. Likewise, in a congregation, there are challenges that can be resolved by using current structures and ways of doing things, such as organizing a young adult Bible study or adding a Saturday-evening worship service geared for families. Adaptive challenges, however, can only be addressed through changes in a person's priorities, habits, values, and/or point of view.

Take the example of Moses in the Old Testament. When it came to leading people through the wilderness, he didn't have a roadmap or a procedures manual. Facing an adaptive challenge, he couldn't look to his toolbox of technical solutions. It took a creative imagination along with guidance from the Almighty to lead an unruly people to the Promised Land. Just so when it comes to leading a congregation to adopt and implement a culture of care, it is not enough to simply change the style of worship, promote yet another Bible study, or even start another outreach program. It takes a new mindset that can adapt to the cultural shifts and contextual challenges of today.

Adaptive leadership requires looking at a changing world with new eyes, being creative and inventive. Consider how people are communicating in new and different ways in a wireless world. It requires adaptive thinking that recognizes that a congregation's website is the new front door, and that effectively communicating with members and neighbors involves embracing the tools of a digital age such as email, text messaging, and social media. It is being open to seeing the church and the world though the lens of adaptive thinking.

Adaptive leadership can help bring about the change that helps a congregation survive and thrive. Heifetz and his colleagues Alexander Grashow and Marty Linsky believe that "new environments and new dreams demand new strategies and abilities, as well as the leadership to mobilize them. As in evolution, these new combinations and variations help organizations thrive under challenging circumstances rather than perish, regress, or contract."[11]

They go on to suggest: "Mobilizing people to meet their immediate adaptive challenges lies at the heart of leadership in the short term. Over time, these and other culture-shaping efforts build an organization's adaptive capacity, fostering processes that will generate new norms that enable the organization to meet the ongoing stream of adaptive challenges posed by a world ever ready to offer new realities, opportunities, and pressures."[12]

The Courage to Make Decisions

Some congregations can become paralyzed when faced with the challenges and change that today's world throws at them. Church leaders may be fearful about making any decisions that "will rock the boat" and make people uncomfortable. Some members may be afraid that things might only get worse, so they hold on to what they know for dear life. This is where faith enters in to remind us that as Christians we are not to be timid but bold in our response. St. Paul reminded the young pastor, Timothy: "For God did not give us a spirit of cowardice, but rather a spirit of power and of love and of self-discipline."[13]

Ron Heifetz and his colleagues suggest three ways that organizations can strengthen their capacity to make tough decisions that come with adaptive change:

1. *Accept that you are going to have to make some tough decisions your whole life.* On the other side of any tough decision facing you, there inevitably will be another one. You can choose to be annoyed or anxious about these choices, or you can embrace them. Tough decisions require you to put your heart into them, nourish the possibilities, and then make a commitment to a course of action.

2. *Nothing is forever.* Rework your decision. If you are struggling with a decision, then all the options likely have some merit. The odds of making the right decision are close to the odds of making the wrong one. Making no decision is a decision in itself.

3. *Tough does not necessarily mean important.* Fortunately, few decisions are so important that everything depends on them. Rarely are the stakes as high as people imagine them to be.[14]

A common complaint of congregational leaders has to do with the length and nature of leadership team meetings. Yet often any suggestion made to change the day, time, or agenda is met with the retort: "but we've always done it that way." It is not unusual for a church leader to report that a council or vestry meeting lasted into the late hours of the night. Or for a pastor to suggest it can be a tense, uncomfortable experience.

A group of church leaders decided to change the approach and format of their governance meetings. They had discovered that 75 percent of their time was spent on reviewing the administration and operations of the congregation, with a heavy dose of church politics thrown in. At the most, 25 percent of the time was devoted to spiritual discernment and care for one another. They took a risk, made a decision, and chose to reverse this approach.

What happened amazed them. By increasing their time spent in spiritual discernment for God's leading and in caring for each other, they found that their meetings were shorter and more productive. They accomplished the same amount of business in ninety minutes that had normally taken three hours. And more importantly, people left the meetings inspired and encouraged rather than drained and discouraged. They also began to operate less from a technical perspective and with a more adaptive, innovative attitude. The following diagram illustrates their changing assumptions.

	Technical Approach	Adaptive Approach
Focus:	75% on administration and politics	75% on personal care and spiritual discernment
	25% on care and discernment	25% on administration and politics
Actions:	1. All reports made in person.	1. Reports can be read ahead of time online.
	2. Everyone needs to weigh in to express a point of view on issues.	2. People check in with others on a personal level. (This often meets the need to be heard.)
	3. Short prayer or scripture reading as traditional part of agenda.	3. Listening to God's Word for guidance. (Bible study connecting with church issues.)

| 4. Open-ended schedule and agenda to honor the business of the church. | 4. Clear agenda with specific timeframe to respect and honor leaders' time commitment. |
| 5. Tyranny of the urgent; vote now and second-guess the outcome. | 5. Take time to process; raise issue once, then wait to vote at the following meeting if possible. |

An Invitation to Be Transformed

God's people are invited to be changed and transformed by Jesus Christ, the Word made flesh. Rather than conform ourselves to the world, we are to allow ourselves to be made new by God's Spirit in baptism. As St. Paul proclaimed to the church in Rome, Christians are to be renewed in mind and spirit to discern what is the will of God—what is good, acceptable, and perfect. As congregations face and maneuver the challenges of change, they are encouraged to do so with spiritual discernment. Decisions are made with prayer and with biblical and theological reflection. Always asking the question: What is God up to? Where is God leading us? What is God's plan for our future?

One of the marks of a healthy, adaptive congregation is the desire to keep learning about the world around them and explore new ways to carry out their ministry. There is an openness to innovation, a willingness to try new things. It is almost certain that congregations will face ongoing challenges and opportunities. And every challenge becomes an opportunity to shape and nurture an adaptive culture that allows God's people to face the future with imagination, confidence, and hope.

Questions for Reflection:

1. Why does change seem so difficult for some people and some organizations?

2. What are some helpful strategies for helping people better deal with change?

3. How does one go about changing the DNA of a congregation?

4. Can you distinguish between a technical problem and an adaptive challenge? How does one approach these two issues differently?

5. What are the three suggestions that enable one to make tough decisions that can lead to cultural change in a congregation?

Notes

1. Wendy Healy, "Our One Constant Is Change," *The Lutheran* (Chicago: The Evangelical Lutheran Church in America, February 2015), 37.

2. Gary Nelson, *Borderland Churches: A Congregation's Introduction to Missional Living* (St. Louis: Chalice, 2008), 126.

3. Adapted from www.wikimediacommons.com [Diffusion of Innovation]. Most diagrams show the last 16% as only laggards; here it has been adapted to include the 2.5% antagonist group.

4. Robert Kegan and Lisa Laskow Lahey, *Immunity to Change: How to Overcome It and Unlock the Potential in Yourself and Your Organization* (Boston: Harvard Business Press, 2009), 50.

5. Ibid., 217.

6. Alan J. Roxburgh, *Missional Map-Making: Skills for Leading in Times of Transition* (San Francisco: Jossey-Bass, 2010), 133.

7. Patricia Sullivan, "The church is not the building. It is our faith and our people." *The Washington Post*, Dec. 26, 2015. http://wjla.com/news/local/100-year-old-arlington-church-sold-to-become-affordable-housing-unit-111159.

8. David C. Laubach, *Twelve Steps to Congregational Transformation: A Practical Guide for Leaders* (Valley Forge, PA: Judson, 2006), 28–29.

9. Kathryn Sime, "Doing More with Less: Congregations Redefine Mission and Ministry with Fewer Members," *The Lutheran Magazine* (online edition), August 2015. Published by the Evangelical Lutheran Church in America. To read more, check out the following link: www.thelutheran.org/article/article.cfm?article_id=12698.

10. Kegan and Lahey, *Immunity to Change*, 29.

11. Ronald Heifetz, Alexander Grashow, and Marty Linsky, *The Practice of Adaptive Leadership: Tools and Tactics for Changing Your Organization and the World* (Boston: Harvard Business Press, 2009), 14.

12. Ibid., 17.

13. 2 Timothy 1:7 NRSV.

14. Heifetz, Grashow, and Linksy, *The Practice of Adaptive Leadership*, 256–57.

4

Contexts of Care

"You shall love the Lord your God with all your heart, and with all your soul, and with all your strength, and with all your mind; and your neighbor as yourself." (Luke 10:22)

A congregation in North Seattle is invested in an adult faith formation process known as the Catechumenate. They follow an ancient practice of preparing people for baptism as well as inviting those who are already baptized to embark on an intentional journey of discipleship. This congregation has been transformed by becoming a community of disciples, and in turn has also helped transform their local neighborhood.

Phinney Ridge Lutheran Church is in the inner city and like many congregations in similar settings, could be in decline. However, just the opposite is true. It adopted the Catechumenate twenty years ago as the means of making disciples. It has become the means for welcoming and integrating new people into the congregation, and the goal is helping people live out their baptism as disciples in daily life. Today more than 75 percent of the congregation has participated in this adult faith formation process. This congregation is growing and thriving. People come from all around the greater Seattle area, drawn to this high-commitment church.

A few years ago the congregation was invited to host Tent City. In the city of Seattle, various churches and other nonprofit agencies agree to let people who are experiencing homelessness camp out on their property for a month or so at a time. This invitation was for the month of December. The pastor and council president brought it to the congregation for conversation. Initially some objected, suggesting that Tent City would be an eyesore, especially during the Advent and Christmas season; it might deter people from coming to worship. Others complained about what would happen to the grounds and the mess that would be left to clean up when Tent City left for another location.

One woman stood up and said she was new to the congregation, having been baptized the previous Easter. She believed that God was calling the congregation to serve the less fortunate. Didn't Jesus say they were to care for the poor and downtrodden? Wasn't this a part of their mission as disciples? Then a young man stood up and remarked: "If we don't do this, then we are all hypocrites. And the whole idea of being a discipleship community is a bunch of bull. Our actions need to match what we say we believe." Unanimous approval followed. Being located in a commercial area, and as a courtesy to their neighbors, the congregation informed the local businesses about their plans.

What happened next is more amazing. The owner of a local hardware store showed up and offered to supply some tents and sleeping bags. A landscape company said they would clean up after and restore the grounds to their original beauty. Then as people arrived and got settled, a local bakery was there to pass out muffins and other baked goods. Every morning the women of the church would provide coffee and juice. The church quilters got into the act and distributed quilts for those chilly December nights. A local Greek restaurant normally closed on Mondays offered to come over on Monday nights to cater a buffet dinner for everyone. Members of the congregation even brought Christmas trees and decorations to help the folks *in Tent City have a more festive holiday season. The larger community joined with the congregation in this simple act of charity and care and became transformed in the process.*

Congregational identity is constructed in part by its context, that is, its relationship to the community in which it finds itself. The context may be rural, urban, or suburban but the issue remains the same, that is, how the congregation is connected to its surrounding community.[1] What relationships have been formed over the years with various organizations and businesses? How do members reflect the makeup of a given neighborhood? How well is a congregation able to respond to opportunities to provide care, as was the case for the folks at Phinney Ridge Lutheran Church?

Many believe that the church in America today is becoming less and less influential in a post-Christian culture. More and more congregations are discovering that one of the ways to reach people with the gospel is through relevant acts of service and care. Churches talk about the importance of caring for people in the community around them but many are unsure of how to effectively meet their needs. Congregations must be willing to go beyond their own church walls and go out into the streets to provide real-life acts of community care.

Rick Rusaw and Eric Swanson describe what they call the Externally Focused Church. They write:

> There is a movement creeping its way across churches of all shapes, sizes, and denominations. It's gaining ground, it's getting attention, and it's making a difference. It's slowly changing church statistics. These churches are evaluating what really matters, and they are reaching skeptical, hurt, and broken people. . . . How are these churches changing the relationship between the church and their communities? How are they getting a skeptical society to hear them? They are externally focused, and this is what defines them:

- They are inwardly strong but outwardly focused.
- They integrate good deeds and good news into the life of the church.
- They value impact and influence in the community more than attendance.
- They seek to be salt, light, and leaven in the community.
- They see themselves as the "soul" of the community.
- They would be greatly missed by the community if they left.[2]

Rusaw and Swanson go on to suggest that vital and effective ministry is not so much measured by what happens inside the walls of the church but rather by the impact the congregation has on its community. "Externally focused churches are internally strong, but they are oriented externally. Their external focus is reflected in those things for which they staff and budget. Because they engage their communities with the good works and good news of Jesus Christ, their communities are better places in which to live. These churches look for ways to be useful to their communities, to be part of their hopes and dreams. They build bridges to their communities instead of walls around themselves."[3]

This chapter argues that internally strong, spiritual congregations—which like Phinney Ridge are marked by growth in discipleship—will live out externally focused Christian vocations in their communities. First, we will discuss how a congregational ministry of discipleship is focused on equipping disciples rather than simply building up membership, as we believe this is the first step in becoming an externally focused congregation. Next, we will identify practical considerations as God, through a process of deepening congregations internally in discipleship, reorients them externally to the world of care around them.

Congregations that seek to be externally focused recognize that their primary purpose is to train and equip disciples. As a discipling center, these congregations then seek to understand the context in which they are called to do ministry. They take time to get to know their neighbors. Congregations as a whole, and sometimes in partnership with others, choose to commit to a common purpose. Finally, they promote a ministry of care in four arenas of life and service.

The Cycle of Discipleship

Jesus talked about his disciples being "in the world" but not "of the world."[4] The Christian has a foot in both the kingdom of God and in the world. One is called to share and emulate the values and spirit of God's kingdom—peace, love, forgiveness, righteousness, healing—by being God's faithful servants in the world while not adopting the ways of the world that are contrary to the gospel.

Congregations are recognizing that the old paradigm of *membership*—creating more church members—needs to be replaced with a new paradigm of *discipleship* if they are to effectively reach out with the gospel beyond the confines of their church walls. "A discipleship model of ministry is focused on Christ's mission of reconciliation to unite all people to God and to one another. Without discipleship training, Christ's mission is too often limited to the confines of the congregation and does not relate sufficiently to one's daily life, let alone to one's encounter with the world."[5]

One of the most important tasks of any congregation is to form and equip disciples to live out their faith in various contexts of care:

In a systems approach to church life, the system has three basic parts: inviting and welcoming, growing and transforming, equipping and sending. One pastor, whose congregation thinks of its purpose as "being and making disciples," said that her congregation sums up its life as "bringing 'em in, growing 'em up, and sending 'em out." In a real sense, this describes the weekly rhythm of the church. We are called and gathered, we are led into God's transforming presence, and then we scatter into the world as God's people. Week by week we are gathered, touched and taught, and then we are sent out.[6]

The Cycle of Discipleship

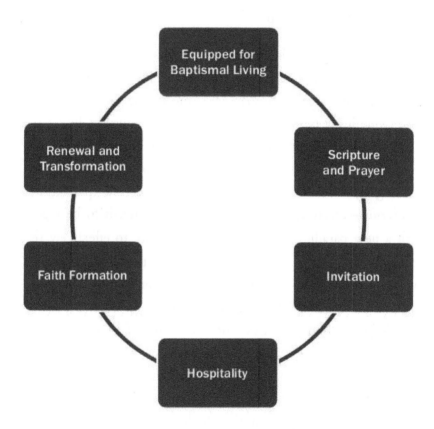

A congregation committed to forming disciples rather than simply making members begins with scripture and prayer. Together the members of a particular faith community study God's word and pray for discernment to determine where God is leading them to serve and who to invite to join them in this adventure of discipleship.

A congregation then extends an invitation to others, including longtime members and those outside the church, to explore discipleship and baptismal living. As people respond to the invitation, the congregation receives them with generous hospitality, welcoming all who desire to join in this journey. A process of intentional faith formation such as the Catechumenate is provided where people can share their faith journey and grow in their relationship with God and each other. This hopefully leads to initiation into the faith (e.g., baptism) or a renewal of one's baptismal covenant with God that brings about transformation into living as a disciple of Jesus. Discipleship is about baptismal living. A congregation of disciples then continues the cycle of making more disciples to serve in their context of care.

Pastor Dietrich Bonhoeffer, theologican and martyr, suggests what it might look like if Christians took seriously the Great Commandment quoted at the beginning of this chapter. "Those who follow Jesus' commandment entirely, who let Jesus' yoke rest on them without resistance, will find the burden they must bear to be light. In the gentle pressure of this yoke they will receive the strength to walk the right path without becoming weary…Where will the call to discipleship lead those who follow it? What decisions and painful separations will it entail? We must take this question to him who alone knows the answer. Only Jesus Christ, who bids us follow him, knows where the path will lead. But we know that it will be a path full of mercy beyond measure. Discipleship is joy."[7]

Understanding the Context

What would it look like if a congregation lived out its common missional purpose in a particular context? One of the important starting points for congregational community care is an understanding of the congregation's connection to those for whom it seeks to provide care in the wider community. This includes a study of demographics to determine such things as the makeup of a given neighborhood in terms of ethnic and religious diversity, socioeconomic status, median age, as well as the number of single and family households. Much of this information is easily obtainable from the local Chamber of Commerce and on the Internet. If a congregation genuinely wishes to reach out to its neighbors, it needs to first know who they are. Specifics on how to learn more about the neighbor will be dealt with in the following chapters.

Where is the congregation located? How does it mirror or differ from the local neighborhood? Have the demographics of the neighborhood changed over the years while the makeup of the congregation has stayed relatively the same? In their excellent book, *Places of Promise: Finding Strength in Your Congregation's Location,* Cynthia Woolever and Deborah Bruce suggest that understanding one's context for ministry is crucial when discerning how to effectively and faithfully engage their communities in ministry. They explore the idea of whether a congregation is either mismatched or well matched to their neighborhood and what the implications are. Some of their findings include the following:

- Communities tend to be more racially diverse than the worshipers in the congregations located there.

- Only a few congregations function as immigrant enclaves—where the majority of worshipers are immigrants in a community where few are immigrants (about 2 percent).

- Many congregations draw a larger percentage of traditional families (married couples with children living at home) than expected, given their community's demographic profile . . .

- Most congregations have a much higher percentage of older

worshipers (sixty-five years of age and older) than the percentage of older people who live in the community.[8]

There are many different contexts of care that congregational leaders will encounter. The neighborhood is but one of them. Contexts of care may also refer to particular circumstances including a crisis such as a neighborhood shooting or a community ravaged by flooding or other natural disasters. A congregation would do well to ask itself: "Where is God calling us to serve in this time and place?" and "How can we bring God's gospel of love, forgiveness, healing, and hope to this particular situation?"

There are also ongoing social issues that may make up the context of care for a given congregation. Some social issues that are rampant today, such as drug and alcohol addiction or spousal and child abuse, occur whether one lives in urban, suburban, small town, or rural contexts. Other issues may be more unique in certain contexts, such as an economic crisis in small towns and rural areas when crops fail or prices plummet or a mill shuts down. It is important that every congregation keep its ear to the ground to better understand the social context in which it is called to minister.

Finally, contexts of care can apply to particular individual or group concerns. The premature death of a high school football star or kidnapping of a child can cause widespread grief and concern among members of the community. What is the role of the congregation in providing solace and hope in a given situation? Transitions in life such as weddings and funerals provide opportunities for community care. A pastor in a small town found himself conducting an increasing number of funeral services. The reason? A local funeral home often calls on him to preside at the funeral of a nonchurched person. He has gained the respect and admiration of many in the community because of his and his congregation's care for the families of the deceased. Some have been led to renew their faith.

Where is a congregation called to serve and provide care? Frederick Buechner is often quoted as saying: "The place God calls you to is the place where your deep gladness and the world's deep hunger meet."[9] Wherever God calls one to serve the neighbor can become a context of care. This is why it is so important to become acquainted with one's neighbors and get to know the needs of the community.

Discovering the Neighbor

Martin Luther suggested that the best way to show one's love for God is to care for the neighbor in need. Once a congregation discovers who their neighbors are, they can begin to build relationships and offer care in appropriate ways. Sometimes it means reviewing their mission plans and their ministry focus if they are to remain faithful to serving the community where God has called them to serve.

Consider the story of Calvary Lutheran Church located in South Minneapolis, Minnesota. Founded in 1923, it had once been a large, thriving congregation whose membership was made up of mostly Scandinavian immigrants and their families. To accommodate their growing congregation, they built a large sanctuary in their present location in 1930, a bold act of faith as contracts were signed the same month as the 1929 stock market crash.

Over the years, the neighborhood became more diverse and many longtime members moved out to the suburbs. Calvary responded to the changes by welcoming people of different races and backgrounds, and providing an emergency food shelf for their neighbors who were struggling economically. In cooperation with the Boys and Girls Club, an evening tutoring program for neighborhood children was begun. Approaching a new millennium, the congregation began significant work in deciding that its commitment was to be outwardly focused and engaged for the sake of the world. Seeking to practice good hospitality and greater inclusivity, Calvary became a Reconciling in Christ congregation that welcomed and affirmed gay, lesbian, bisexual, and transgender individuals and their families.

On the eve of their seventy-fifth anniversary, the congregation proclaimed their intention to remain in their present location and serve the people of their neighborhood by raising a banner reading "In the City for Good." That banner remains on the outside of the church tower for all to see. The church building now houses a variety of service organizations including the Urban Arts Academy founded by Calvary that provides after-school and summer enrichment programs for the neighborhood children. Grade-school children from a variety of socioeconomic and ethnic backgrounds gather on weekdays for classes in art, music, cooking, and drama, as well as tutoring. The church and the academy host a Gala every year that raises money so that every child who wishes to participate is able to attend regardless of their ability to pay.

Today about 125 members gather on a given Sunday for worship; and at least twenty-five of those who are under the age of ten come forward for the children's sermon. The worshipers are as diverse as the neighborhood. Calvary may be small but it is spiritually strong, and it continues to serve a changing neighborhood in its commitment to the gospel and to social justice.

The above illustrates how one congregation made an effort to get to know their neighbors, authentically connecting with them, building relationships, and bringing new life to both congregation and community. Calvary's story can serve as a guide for other congregations who seek to connect with their neighbors in a meaningful way. This is especially true in diverse neighborhoods where the context of care can be somewhat complex as noted below:

Healing and transformative care in diverse communities requires attention to the needs of all persons in the communities, indigenous peoples, immigrants, newcomers, long-term residents, Muslims, Christians, and Jews. This care must keep in mind both the needs of the individuals and the broader needs of the community, as well as our faith commitment to the life-giving use of power and the vision of a peaceful diverse society in which all life flourishes. A pastoral care perspective can be a helpful lens with which to address diversity. . . . Meaningful and healthy engagement across difference requires first an environment of care and respect for all involved, Christians and non-Christians, newcomers and old-timers, or Euro-Americans, Native Americans, Latina/os, and African Americans, the whole community.[10]

A willingness to explore the world of the neighbor beyond our church walls is critical. It will not only help us better understand the needs of our neighbor but we may find ourselves changed in the process. Gary Nelson, in his book *Borderland Churches: A Congregations Introduction to Missional Living*, suggests that such places as neighborhoods, workplaces, and community sports leagues are essential places where one lives the faith and gets to know the needs of the neighbor. He writes:

To truly engage our neighbors, we must "see" them, recognize their difference, honor their uniqueness, and respect the intrinsic values they keep whether or not we agree with them. The eyes that "see" emerge from the conscious willingness to embed ourselves in the network of relationships set before us. . . . Embedding is a place of mutual sharing that provides the possibilities of progressing into a deeper living commitment of understanding. This can be quite unsettling for a variety of reasons. We may be changed by the encounters. We may learn things about ourselves and about the other that causes us to transform our beliefs and practices.[11]

A willingness to be transformed by the other can bring enormous freedom. It enables us to set aside our preconceived notions and to enter into civil conversation and genuine dialogue with others.

Alan Roxburgh suggests this will "require radically different ways of thinking about being the church in our day. For one thing, it's going to mean learning how to actually listen to people without making them objects of our ends. It's going to mean a readiness to enter into dialogue with the other, seeking to listen to their stories and conversations in a genuinely human engagement. This is going to feel very strange and disrupting for many Christians, even those in leadership, because it will mean we are no longer in control of the conversation."[12]

Committing to a Common Purpose

One of the ways to help a congregation connect with and respond to its particular context is to identify a common purpose or issue that requires the congregation's attention. The issue of immigration, for example, has become a critical issue for many in this country and has had a particular impact on those living in the Southwest. Several churches in Tucson, Arizona have joined together in providing services to people threatened with deportation as well as offering humanitarian aid to people attempting to cross the border between Mexico and the United States. A number of them, in fact, have become part of the sanctuary movement offering a safe refuge for individuals and families targeted as "illegals."

These same churches are partnering with other organizations that have been formed to address the issues of deportation and border crossings. Some of those include the Humane Border Project, Border Links, and No More Deaths/No Mas Muertes. Their purpose is fourfold: a) to educate the public on what the issues are, b) to offer legal assistance to people threatened with deportation, c) to provide emergency aid (such as food, water, blankets, etc.) to those suffering in the desert south of the border, and d) to help change immigration laws and procedures.

Below is an excerpt from *Bishops on the Border: Pastoral Responses to Immigration* that highlight some of the humanitarian concerns that the Tucson congregations are seeking to address. Bishop Minerva G. Carcano of the United Methodist Church shares about her visit to the border:

> We walked and worked with persons who have committed their lives to extending care to immigrants in the desert. It is not an uncommon experience for immigrants to find themselves stranded in the desert either because they have been injured on the arduous immigrant journey or by being separated from the group with whom they were traveling. Sometimes they travel alone, running out of water and food and becoming too weak to continue. . . . Three hundred immigrants were dying every year in Arizona's border desert.[13]

One of the book's key questions is "Why does society continue to allow migrant workers to die in the desert?" Another critical question has to do with why our society is so quick to demonize those who cross our borders in search of a better and safer life, which in some cases can mean survival.

These same church leaders refer to scripture passages that speak of hospitality to the stranger, such as "You shall not wrong or oppress a resident alien, for you were aliens in the Land of Egypt."[14] They appeal to congregations to welcome the stranger, serve the oppressed, and accompany the unfortunate. It's all about overcoming obstacles in order "to create access and availability to God's unconditional love for and forgiveness to the least, the last, the lost, and the little."[15]

There are many other societal concerns that congregations may discover in the context of their own communities, especially those related to issues of equality and economic justice. Poverty and homelessness are among the issues facing many communities. As a congregation determines what concerns need to be addressed in their ministry context, they would do well to consider how God is calling them to be Christ among their neighbors. Where and how is God leading them to serve and extend Christ-like care to others?

Four Arenas of Care

The vocation of a Christian is to live out one's baptism in the various arenas of life. Martin Luther identified four areas where one is called to share their faith in word and in deed: a) home and family, b) the workplace, c) the neighborhood, and d) the public arena and the wider world.[16] These become the contexts where today's disciples carry out their ministry in daily life, using their gifts to serve the neighbor.

The context of home and family: Individuals and congregations share a calling to support the basic human institutions of home and family, in whatever forms they exist. This includes making the home a safe place physically, emotionally, and spiritually. The family context is where the love of God is shared with one's closest neighbor: a spouse, a child, a housemate, and others who are part of one's intimate circle. The home is where faith, values, and right living are taught, nurtured, and practiced among loved ones. It is also the place where basic needs such as food, clothing, and shelter are provided.

The context of the workplace: In Luther's view, there is no difference in stature between a bishop and a cobbler. Each one is called to minister to others: the bishop with oversight and support of pastors, and the cobbler by using one's tools to make the best shoes he can for the customer. Many people fail to understand the simple truth that everyone is called to a ministry of some kind. The workplace can be viewed as a context in which to extend God's loving care to others.

College students attended a class on vocation as ministry. Field trips were taken to meet with people in their workplace. For example, a visit to the hospital included visits with chaplains, doctors, and nurses to hear how each one saw their work as an extension of God's care. In another instance, a visit to an army base included conversations with a military chaplain, an officer, and an enlisted man who all saw what they did as a ministry. Students were transformed by this experience. They discovered that whatever one's workplace—in the fields of education, business, medicine, sanitation, public service, and the like—it can be considered a place to do ministry as one serves God by serving and caring for others.

The context of the neighborhood: Friends and neighbors are part of our circle of care. They may have particular needs that one may or may not be aware of. Jesus tells a story of someone who needed a loaf of bread and hounded his neighbor, a judge, much of the night to help him. Exasperated, the judge finally came out from his home and gave his neighbor the bread. While this parable is about being persistent in prayer, it also gives us a clue on how one is to treat the neighbor.

Should the need be made clear, the Christian is called to determine if she or he has the means to help and then to assist in whatever way God leads them to care for others. It may be offering a meal to someone who is home from the hospital, bringing flowers to a neighbor who has lost a loved one, offering to provide transportation for someone who is homebound, of being a friend to someone who is lonely. All acts of charity done in a spirit of love can be a reflection of God's love and care for the neighbor in need.

The context of the public arena and wider world: Christians are also called to make a difference in the world. This may mean standing up for issues of economic or social justice in the larger community. It may involve running for public office in order to make laws and policies more equitable. It might even lead one to participate in a protest movement of those seeking a particular change, even when it is not a popular thing to do. Living in the covenant of one's baptism is about standing up for the values that are shaped by one's faith, which then often propels one into the public arena.

Much more will be said about these last two contexts of care—neighborhood and the larger community in which an individual or congregation is located—in upcoming chapters. Contexts of care are complex, continually changing, and present many occasions for the development of congregational care beyond church walls. See illustration below.[17]

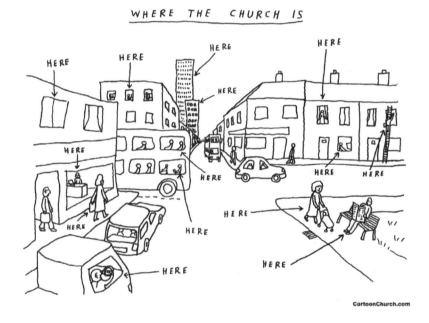

Who Is My Neighbor?

There is a growing awareness in the church, within the context of the congregation, of the need for care of the stranger and the newcomer. Jessicah Duckworth, in her book *Wide Welcome: How the Unsettling Presence of Newcomers Can Save the Church*, explores the importance of congregations paying attention to the strangers and newcomers in their midst. "Newcomers call the church to its task of 'making disciples.' Making disciples is the life-sustaining, life-saving work that makes up the church's identity. The church does not seek permanence with established membership as the solid foundation, but fluidity and movement of newcomers and established members together. Thus, the life of the church depends upon a newcomer's presence within the body of Christ."[18]

Those who gather as church in the name of Jesus are a holy people, the called-out people of God. As such, the focus of their worship and ministry needs to consider not just those on the inside, but those on the outside as well. Gordon Lathrop writes: "If the meeting constitutes just us as the insiders, then Christian holiness involves the subversion of the meeting. . . . The practice of holiness involves the constant work on the open door, both that all others may come in and that what is seen in the liturgy may flow out. The practice of holiness is the discovery of God's gift to all of us, together."[19]

Strangers and newcomers can, in fact, be another context of care. They may be searching for community, greater meaning in life, and/or a deeper relationship with God. They can also breathe new life into a congregation, bringing a fresh perspective and helping the congregation see with new eyes the opportunities for ministry around them. "Congregations of hope are realized through the newcomers who come and 'be-come' participants within communities of practice. Without newcomers, communities die; they turn in on themselves and away from the Other, the stranger, and the world God loves. At the same time, these newcomer strangers lurk threateningly, representing by their presence a hope for a new community that requires a death of the old. . . . Welcoming the Other and the stranger molds and shapes who we are and who we are to become. This dying and rising represents a radical reorientation to the world God loves."[20]

Contexts of care are all around us. Congregations need only look beyond their walls to see the many opportunities God has set before them. Whether it be individuals in need or a community in crisis, God is calling the church to be Christ's presence of hope and healing. The context of care is wherever we encounter the neighbor in need. Returning to the scripture quoted at the beginning of this chapter, we recall Jesus' admonition to love our neighbor as our self. When Jesus was asked by a lawyer, "Who is my neighbor?," Jesus told the parable of the Good Samaritan. Upon finishing his story, Jesus asked the lawyer to identify the one who was neighbor to the one who was robbed. The man answered, "The one who showed him mercy." Jesus said to him, "Go and do likewise."[21]

Questions for Reflection:

1. How is a congregation's identity shaped by the community around it?

2. Why is it important for a congregation to get to know their neighbors?

3. How might you discover opportunities God is providing for your congregation to engage more deeply in your community?

4. Can you think of some societal issues that your community is wrestling with? How might your congregation contribute to the conversation? How might it become involved?

5. Describe how Luther's four areas of care are present in your particular community context. What avenues for congregational community care do they suggest?

Notes

1. See also Jeanne Hoeft, L. Shannon Jung, and Joretta Marshall, *Practicing Care in Rural Congregations and Communities* (Minneapolis: Fortress Press, 2013), 32–33.

2. Rick Rusaw and Eric Swanson, *The Externally Focused Church* (Loveland, CO: Group Publishing, 2004), 12.

3. Ibid., 17.

4. John 17:6-26.

5. Robert Schmalzle with Aaron Schmalzle, *The 7 Habits of Jesus: A Faith Formation Handbook for Discipleship* (Kissimmee, FL: New Life Publishing, 2014), 19.

6. Anthony B. Robinson, *Changing the Conversation: A Third Way for Congregations* (Grand Rapids, MI: Eerdmans, 2008), 143.

7. Dietrich Bonhoeffer. *Discipleship*, Dietrich Bonhoeffer Works, Vol. 4. Minneapolis: Fortress Press, 2001, pp. 39–40.

8. Cynthia Woolever and Deborah Bruce, *Places of Promise: Finding Strength in Your Congregation's Location* (Louisville: Westminster John Knox, 2008), 63–65.

9. Frederick Buechner, Wishful Thinking: A Theological ABC (New York: Harper, 1982).

10. Hoeft, Jung, and Marshall, *Practicing Care in Rural Congregations and Communities*, 101.

11. Gary V. Nelson, *Borderland Churches: A Congregation's Introduction to Missional Living* (St. Louis: Chalice, 2008), 120.

12. Alan J. Roxburgh, *Missional: Joining God in the Neighborhood* (Grand Rapids: Baker, 2011), 141.

13. Mark Adams, Minerva G. Carcano, Gerald Kicanas, Kirk Smith, and Stephen Talmage, *Bishops on the Border: Pastoral Responses to Immigration* (New York: Morehouse, 2013), 10–11.

14. Exodus 22:21-22. See also Deut. 10:17-19 and Lev. 19:33-34.

15. Adams et al., *Bishops on the Border*, 84.

16. Martin Luther.

17. Illustration by Dave Walker. Used with permission.

18. Jessicah Duckworth, *Wide Welcome: How the Unsettling Presence of Newcomers Can Save the Church* (Minneapolis: Fortress Press, 2014), 4.

19. Gordon W. Lathrop, *Holy People: A Liturgical Ecclesiology* (Minneapolis: Fortress Press, 2006), 211.

20. Duckworth, *Wide Welcome*, 108.

21. Luke 10:25-37.

5

Creating Care Communities

If a brother or sister is naked and lacks daily food, and one of you says to them, "Go in peace; keep warm, and eat your fill," and yet you do not supply their bodily needs, what is the good of that? So faith by itself, if it has no works, is dead. (James 2:15-17)

It was the summer of 1990, just prior to the start of the Gulf War, and the U.S. government was threatening to bomb Iraq for its invasion of the neighboring country of Kuwait. People in the community were uneasy about the notion of going to war in the desert. Protestors assembled at the Federal Building in Seattle to make a stand for peace. Some members of my Northwest congregation asked if we might consider having a prayer service at our church.

A good friend of mine, Brian "Red" Burchfield, and his wife had just returned from South Africa where they had been serving as co-pastors and been advocates for an end to Apartheid in that country. He had been an intern pastor at our congregation years before, so many members had followed his career, maintaining deep affection and respect for him. I asked him if he would preach at a "Prayer for Peace" service to be held at our church the following Sunday night, and he agreed.

We sent word out through the community by way of newspaper articles, radio, and word of mouth. (This was before Facebook and other social media.) Members of the congregation invited their friends and neighbors to join them for this special worship service. On Sunday night the sanctuary was packed to overflowing. One could sense both the fear of war and the hope for peace that was in the air.

We had prepared a simple liturgy for peace, including hymns and scripture. Pastor Burchfield delivered a powerful sermon on his experience in South Africa as he worked for justice and supported nonviolence as a peaceful approach to a solution there. The crowd was mesmerized as he spoke and applied his insight to the current political situation in the Middle East. Following his sermon, people were invited to come forward and light a candle for peace, placing them in a box of sand that sat on a table in front of the altar while the congregation sang a hymn. It was moving to see so many people come forward.

The event had touched a nerve in members of the congregation and in the community. People had come together around a common cause. And the church had responded to a felt need in the larger community around it, offering a space and means of care for those concerned about issues of peace and the value of human life.

Creating a caring community is no simple task. Despite the tension some pastors feel between congregational caregiving and leading in mission, most congregations are fairly good at caring for members of their own community of faith. Clergy are trained in pastoral care to provide counseling and other assistance in times of need. Lay members are often trained in how to deliver care to those within the sphere of the congregation who need assistance, whether it be taking communion to shut-ins, offering rides to church for those who need transportation, doing chores for the homebound, providing meals for the sick, and offering consolation for those experiencing grief, heartache, or other difficult life transitions. However, as we have indicated before in this book, caregiving is not limited to those "inside" the church walls.

There is a world aching for God's healing and redemptive love. The challenge is to help congregations recognize that care extends to the larger community and that such caregiving is an expression of faith. As the verse from James suggests, faith is made real and shows itself in works of love and care for others. The overall purpose of this chapter is to suggest various components of care that a congregation might consider developing. To that end, we will explore the following: 1) creating a culture of care, 2) determining a biblical basis for action, 3) assessing the resources needed for care, 4) reviewing and considering various types of care, and 5) communicating the need for and promoting acts of care.

Create a Culture of Care

Many church leaders understand that they are called to partner with God in a mission of healing for the sake of the world and desire to engage their congregation in this great work. Before seeking to move the congregation in a missional (outward) direction, they would do well to first check the climate of their congregation. Is the congregation healthy? Health implies a strong focus on spiritual practices, a high level of trust in leadership, a minimal amount of manageable conflict, positive relationships among members, and a reasonably sound economic base.

Another important consideration has to do with the culture of the congregation. From what values does a congregation operate? Is the congregation focused inward on itself or also outward toward the world? How do members of the congregation view outsiders? Is there a spirit of genuine hospitality where all are truly welcome?

The following diagram is designed to help church leaders assess a congregation's relationship with its community and its perspective on care.

QUADRANTS OF CARE

In quadrant 1, we have a congregation that focuses its resources of care primarily on itself, its own members. In quadrant 2, we have a congregation that desires to care for their neighbors, but without understanding the context and the real, felt needs of the community around them. For example, members of a congregation may open a food pantry for their neighbors when the real need may be affordable housing.

Quadrant 3 is a congregation that understands its context and seeks to address the needs of those outside its church family by a) providing funds for special causes such as world hunger or b) inviting their neighbors into the life and ministry of the congregation where they might avail themselves of the services of care offered to members. They are not aware of how to take the resources of care out into their community or how to nurture relationships with their neighbors.

Finally, in quadrant 4, we see a congregation that is passionate about reaching out to its community and is committed to issues of justice and social change. They are involved in worthwhile projects such as Habitat for Humanity. But they fail to develop personal relationships of care with members of their community.

All of these types of congregations have merit; and yet the *missional congregation* seeks a healthy balance of all four, ending up at the center of the diagram. This is a congregation that sees the importance of going out, listening, and developing personal relationships. It understands the context—the larger community with its felt problems and challenges—in which it is called to do ministry. It takes time to assess what kinds of care may be appropriate to offer in a given situation. And it nurtures those in the congregation—providing care and equipping them for service in the wider world.

An example of such a congregation that endeavors to find such a balance is the Church of the Beloved, an ELCA congregation in Edmonds, Washington. They have taken a unique approach, through music, to making the gospel come alive to congregants and to members of the larger community. Michael Brenner in his article in *Seeds for the Parish* reports:

Beloved's uniqueness was deliberate from its beginning. The congregation's genesis came in 2004, when a committee attempted to address declining church attendance. The statistics were particularly discouraging in the Seattle area—only six percent of people attended church regularly.

The initial focus was the millennial generation, but the [vision] committee soon found itself targeting a mindset rather than a demographic. Their vision as a new congregation developed around creative, experiential worship and striving to create a sense of community in a diverse and fragmented society . . .

As the congregation embraces new opportunities their community ministry coordinator, Jacqueline Cuayo, plays a vital role in facilitating communication between [music] groups and church members, between the congregation and the community. And her work with the creative and theological direction of the congregation also involves facilitating and passing information from one place to another and helping people connect.

"We are a group of people that want to worship God and follow the way of Jesus in a way that we can connect to in a modern day language," said Jacqueline. "How do we say the same thing, but in a way that traditional and non-religious people might connect with it?"[1]

The Church of the Beloved is a congregation that is continually looking for ways to connect with the members of the larger community around it. Reaching out to music groups and offering the kind of worship that speaks to those outside the congregation is but one way they are seeking to make a difference in people's lives. Their care for members is not a means to an end but rather a means for creating more disciples to help them reach out to others with the gospel of God's love in a way that communicates and connects to the various life situations of others. In doing so, congregational leaders attempt to take into account all four of the *quadrants of care*: congregation, community, context, and care for others.

Church leaders who want to create a climate of care would do well to contemplate where their congregation is located in the *quadrants of care*. It may also be helpful to examine the various areas of congregational ministry in an attempt to assess both the climate and the culture of their community of faith. This is important in determining a congregation's readiness for mission and how many of their members have an aptitude for providing community care. *See the Appendix for a Ministry Assessment Survey.*

Explore a Biblical Basis for Action

It goes without saying that a congregation that is serious about partnering with God in the healing of and care for the world must steep itself in scripture and in prayer. Congregations that believe in *the making of disciples for the sake of the world* promote spiritual practices that help people live out their faith in daily life. Congregations that are willing to be transformed by God's Spirit are bold in exploring the Bible for guidance and in praying for discernment of where God is leading them to serve.

Some congregations have chosen to use the term *disciple* instead of *member* to indicate that Christianity is not simply about joining an organization. Rather it is about being a disciple of Jesus in daily life. But simply changing the designation does not make it so. In his book *The 7 Habits of Jesus*, Robert Schmalzle describes seven spiritual practices that he believes are attributes of discipleship.[2]

Spiritual practices include such things as regular worship, Bible reading, prayer, and care. They become marks of discipleship that take many forms, as illustrated, for example, in a practical resource called *Animate Practices* featuring people like Brian McLaren, Mike Slaughter, and Phyllis Tickle.[3] When a congregation encourages and practices spiritual disciplines, it can transform not only the individual but the entire community of faith. Michael Foss writes: "When the marks of discipleship are adopted and practiced by an individual, growth happens. When adopted and practiced by a group of individuals, greater growth happens, because of the mutual encouragement, reinforcement, and support that comes from common commitment . . . when adopted by the whole congregation and practiced by many, a climate of change is introduced, an atmosphere of excitement and expectation prevails."[4]

The passage from James at the beginning of this chapter suggests that faith should show itself in action. Spiritual practices by themselves are not some new form of works righteousness, for one does not earn God's favor or salvation by adopting certain practices. Rather they are the marks of a living faith and of a church faithful to its calling: to serve God and the world in need. Martin Luther taught that we are not saved *by* our good works but we are saved *in order to do* good works. This is what we call grace-filled living, acting out of gratitude to God who has blessed us with such grace.

One telling passage of scripture that can guide a congregation in acts of care for the neighbor is from the first letter of St. John:

> Beloved, let us love one another, because love is from God; everyone who loves is born of God and knows God. Whoever does not love does not know God, for God is love. God's love was revealed among us in this way: God sent his only Son into the world so that we might live through him. In this is love, not that we loved God but that he loved us and sent his Son to be the atoning sacrifice for our sins. Beloved, since God loved us so much, we also ought to love one another . . .
>
> We love because he first loved us. Those who say, "I love God," and hate their brothers or sisters, are liars; for those who do not love a brother or sister whom they have seen, cannot love God whom they have not seen. The commandment we have from him is this: those who love God must love their brothers and sisters also.[5]

This scripture reminds us that we are to care for those closest to us. It includes loving members of our immediate family and members of our family of faith. But the love of God reaches beyond these circles of care to include so many more. Whenever we see a neighbor in need, we meet a brother or sister for whom we are called to love and care. Their race, creed, sexual orientation, or economic status shouldn't matter. The New Testament is clear that the guiding force of all should be love.

God reminded Abraham that God's people were "blessed to be a blessing."[6] The Bible seems clear that the church is not an end in itself; rather it exists to serve God's larger purpose, sharing a gospel of love and healing for the sake of the world. "The newness of God is framed in our call as the church to be representatives of the new way of living together: a way of life bounded by love and service to one another and the willingness to pour ourselves out into the world . . . to display what life as the forgiven and forgiving people of God is really like."[7]

Assess Resources and Assets of Care

Is the cup half empty or half full? Some congregations operate with a theology of scarcity. They may understand the deep needs in a given community and even desire to help. But what holds them back is the belief that they do not have the resources to offer care where it is most needed. In their view, they lack the funding, the volunteers, the leadership, and whatever else may be necessary to effectively address the particular concerns of their neighborhood.

Other congregations, on the other hand, view the same challenges with a theology of abundance. They believe that God has given them all the resources they need to be faithful to God's call to care for their neighbor. They have been blessed with God's grace, the gifts of God's people, visionary leadership, and financial opportunity. They believe the truth of St. Paul's words: "God is able to provide you with every blessing in abundance, so that by always having enough of everything, you may share abundantly in every good work."[8]

It is my belief that God has given every congregation all the gifts and blessings it needs to carry out the work God is calling them to do in their community context. Asset mapping is a good place for most congregations to start when determining if and how they might respond to a given need for care in their community. This means taking stock of all the gifts and resources with which a congregation has been blessed. The leadership of a congregation may choose to invite members to join in the following exercise. Below is a list of questions that may help reveal even some of the hidden blessings:

1. What are the spiritual blessings we have been given from God?
2. What do we do well? What are some of the strengths of this congregation?
3. What talents and expertise do we find both explicit and hidden among our members?
4. How might our physical facilities be used to meet the needs of our neighbors?
5. What is the financial potential of member contributions to our ministry? (Note that this does not limit the amount to current giving patterns.)
6. How might current budgeted funds be repurposed for new outreach opportunities that help us care more effectively for members in our community?

Building on one's strengths is an important concept in mapping assets. Too many congregations think they need to be "all things to all people" and end up getting discouraged because they don't seem to have enough resources (e.g., volunteers and money) to do it all. Rather taking an inventory of the strengths of a congregation and then discovering how to build on those strengths is a more strategic and effective path to follow. This is illustrated by the story below.

Prince of Peace in Phoenix, Arizona ran a popular daycare and preschool program that brought in two hundred children to campus every weekday. As the leadership discovered that the demographics in the neighborhood showed it was made up mostly of young families and that many of the families of preschool children were unchurched, they chose to build on their reputation for early childhood education. They invited members of the community to join their preschool families on campus for various events including "trunk-or-treat" (families sharing Halloween treats from their cars in the church parking lot), a Saturday Easter egg hunt, an outdoor movie family night, and so on. They strategized to start an after-school program for latchkey children and a summer camp on their campus for young children in the neighborhood.

The church is the called-out people of God. We are called together in order to go out into the world with the healing gift of the gospel. In order to be faithful to that calling, a congregation may find it necessary to reorder its priorities and repurpose its resources. "Living, no matter how haltingly, as an alternative, countercultural, biblical community of reconciliation is the call of God's reign. Recovering our missional soul will probably mean stopping as many things that we usually think of as church as it means starting new ones. The ongoing process of consolidating our lives so we can actually live in community as God's people under his reign will be the difficult work."[9]

Church leaders are encouraged to do the "grow, hold, and fold" exercise as they consider how to spend their resources of people and money in carrying out their ministry in a given community. First, they must determine where they would like to grow their ministry—what new mission opportunity has God set before them? Next, they consider what ministries they need to hold on to and continue to nurture. What is it they are already doing that is important to keep doing in order to be faithful to their mission? Finally, it is important to discern what ministries to fold. What are those good things that have run their course that can be celebrated and put to bed? What is it that no longer serves the larger purpose and how can those resources be redirected? The latter is perhaps the hardest of all to do. Keep in mind that everything—including staff and programs—have a life cycle.[10]

Consider Types of Care

Components of care include various types of caregiving. This applies to both individuals and to the corporate life of a congregation. Types of care also depend on the context and situation. For example, counseling can refer to an *individual* who may be going through a divorce, a *couple* who is planning their marriage, or even a *group or community* who have endured a shared tragedy or are facing a difficult decision like war as illustrated in the opening story of this chapter.

Congregations who seek to provide care for their neighbors in the larger community should first consider whether the situation calls for an individual act of care or a corporate act of care. Who is affected by a given situation? How many people are in need of care? What is the circumstance that calls for pastoral and community care? In the next chapter, we will explore more deeply how congregations might engage in collaborative acts of care in partnership with others in the community.

An example of this is the corporate grieving process that was established for the people of Trinity Lutheran in the Greater Seattle area following the loss of their campus to an arson fire. Realizing that church staff and members of all ages needed an outlet for dealing with their grief and anger, people were invited to attend small-group sessions held in various homes, with a trained counselor to guide the conversation. At one such gathering a mother related to the group that her five-year-old daughter had colored an egg carton with red and orange crayons and then cut it into shreds. "There Mommy," she said, "that is what is left of our church." Recognizing that people needed to be together to share their feelings and pray for one another, the pastoral leadership promoted this opportunity as an important step toward healing. The congregation later expanded upon this and invited other victims of arson as well as neighboring congregations in the area to join with them in a community-wide worship service of healing.

Specific types of community care can be described as follows: a) counseling, b) spiritual direction, c) standing with a person or persons in time of need, d) providing a service of care, e) offering a ritual of care, f) making items of necessity available, g) congregation-based community organizing, and h) working for socioeconomic justice appropriate to a given community. A helpful resource in determining appropriate types of care is David Switzer's book, *Pastoral Care Emergencies*.[11]

Counseling is providing deep listening to individuals, families, and groups in the community. It offers an opportunity to address mutual concerns such as illustrated by the Trinity story above. The goal is to help people explore what is on their hearts and minds, and perhaps decide what action to take next that could help them find a solution to a problem and/or move forward with their lives.

Spiritual Direction differs from counseling in that the directee—the person seeking direction—is invited to consider how God is at work in his or her life and in a given situation. The director asks such questions as "What is God up to here?" and "Where is God leading you?" The goal is to help a person or persons—in the case of group spiritual direction—discern where faith connects with life and how one might enter into God's promised future.

Standing with someone is a show of empathy, being with another in times of pain or difficulty. Some call it *practicing presence* for others by offering support by simply being present. As a parish pastor, I recall being called to the home of a mother who had lost her child to crib death. The child was to be baptized the following Sunday. The father was out of town and the woman was alone with her grief. I hugged her as she sobbed, mumbled something like "sorry for your loss," and then we sat in silence for a while, neither one of us knowing what to say. I believe I finally read Psalm 23 and prayed with her. Later I apologized for not offering more words of solace, and the young mother responded that just my presence was a great comfort. Another example was standing with a repentant arsonist—who had burned down our church—at his sentencing hearing. I was called to testify on his behalf as to his character while members of our church leadership team were simply present in the courtroom to offer their support for this troubled young man.

Providing a service of care takes many forms, such as offering to provide transportation for a group of shut-ins who wish to attend worship or to go shopping. It may mean setting up an employment-counseling network in an area where there is high unemployment. It could be an after-school program for neighborhood children known as latchkey kids.

Offering a ritual of care will be dealt with in more detail in chapter seven. It may be appropriate for a congregation to consider offering a rite to mark some of the transitions in life, such as: a) at the conception of a child, a birth, an adoption, or miscarriage; b) for an engagement, marriage, or divorce; c) when one loses a job or begins retirement; d) when one goes into the armed services or returns from active service; or e) a time of serious illness, when one is dying, and celebrating one's life after death.

Making items available to meet the felt needs of a community is another act of care. This might take the form of establishing a food or clothing pantry, particularly in a low-income area. It could mean collecting household items in order to help furnish the apartment of a refugee family. Another example is from an eight-year-old girl who decided that for her birthday she and her friends would put together "survival kits" for the homeless in their community. They included bottles of water, toiletries, and nonperishable food items. These children were given a citation of appreciation from a local organization that provides a ministry to people on the street who have no home.

Congregation-based community organizing is another way to offer care in collaboration and cooperation with other congregations and organizations in the community. This will be explored in detail in chapter eight. This concept suggests that congregations can make more of an impact if they join with other partners in making care available to the community at large.

Working for socioeconomic justice is an act of community care that can help make a difference for good in a given community. In one community, there may be the need for reforming the criminal justice or penal system. In another community, it may mean lobbying the local government and area businesses to provide jobs and a living wage especially where there is economic disparity. In yet another community, it may include working for greater acceptance and equality among various ethnic and religious groups. See chapter nine, "Ministry on the Margins," which deals with multicultural and intercultural diversity in church and community.

Promote Acts of Care

Having discerned along with their congregation what God is calling and inviting them to do, church leaders have a responsibility for helping members focus on this new vision. This may be part of a mission outreach plan that they believe will help the congregation move forward in a missional direction. And without a sense of "buy-in" by the members of that community of faith, the activity envisioned may never happen.

Leadership needs to find a way to communicate the need and the plan for care effectively, as well as to build a sense of ownership among their members for the vision. Chapter ten is devoted to a mode of strategic planning process that involves the whole congregation from the beginning. It is important to both listen to what the Spirit is saying through God's people as well as to educate them as to the needs for care in their community. There are some practical ways to promote opportunities for care that include the following:

1. The congregation's leadership needs to be forthcoming about some of the priorities of care that have been determined by their deep listening to members of the church and community. For it is together they will discern where God is leading them.

2. Various means of communication such as the Sunday bulletin, weekly newsletter, and periodic temple talks at worship can be helpful.

3. Sermons are a good way to help a congregation consider the biblical, theological, and practical reasons for embracing a particular cause.

4. Technology is an important tool that can provide information to members of church and community alike through an up-to-date website and the effective use of emails, Facebook, Twitter, etc.

5. Foster a spirit of imagination among members of the congregation. Suggest it is okay to try new things and give them the freedom to fail. This will encourage some to get outside of their comfort zone.

God calls the church out into the world, beyond church walls, to be the new people of God. David Augsburger reminds us: "The church is an alternative community—an alternative to human communities that live by coercion, competition, and collective self-interest. It seeks to be a community of disciples who obey the particular ways of God that are revealed in Jesus. It models neighbor love, transformative redemptive justice, inclusion of the stranger, servanthood to each other and beyond, creative love, forgiveness and reconciliation and the humility to recognize and confess its own need for repentance and forgiveness."[12]

The following diagram offers a summary of the cycle of care as described in this chapter.

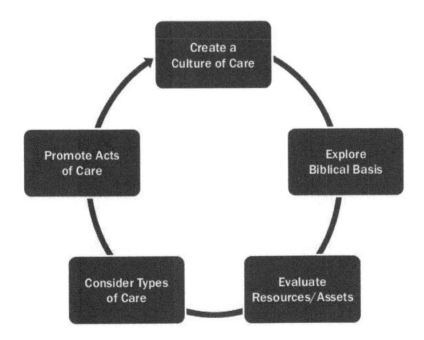

The Cycle of Care

An offertory prayer used on the third Sunday in Advent in many congregations expresses the desire of God's people to enter into this cycle of care. "God of abundance, we bring before you the precious fruits of your creation, and with them our very lives. Teach us patience and hope as we care for all of those in need as we await your promised reign, through your beloved, Jesus Christ. Amen."[13] For it is in caring for others that the light of Christ shines brightly in our world.

Creating caring communities is more than just encouraging members to care for each other within the community of faith. It is looking beyond church walls at the needs, issues, and challenges of the day facing people in the neighborhood and the wider world. It means encouraging a congregation to enter into a cycle of care that is biblically based, makes good use of the gifts and passion of congregational members, takes into account many different kinds of care, and finally encourages and equips people to carry out this ministry of care in daily life.

Questions for Reflection:

1. What are the four elements in the quadrants of care? How might this tool be helpful in determining a congregation's perspective on pastoral and community care?

2. How can Bible study and prayer be helpful in discerning where God is leading a congregation to serve in its community?

3. Why is it important to map the assets and resources of a congregation?

4. Describe some types of care a congregation might consider providing to their neighbors.

5. Describe how the Cycle of Care continues to nurture and promote a climate of care.

Notes

1. Michael Brenner, "Saying Yes to Opportunities for Ministry," *Seeds for the Parish: Resource Paper for Leaders of ELCA Congregations* (Winter 2015): 1.

2. Robert Schmalzle with Aaron Schmalzle, *The 7 Habits of Jesus: A Faith Formation Handbook for Discipleship* (Nottingham, UK: New Life Publishing, 2014).

3. *Animate Practices* (Minneapolis: Spark House, 2014).

4. Michael Foss, *Power Surge: Six Marks of Discipleship for a Changing Church* (Minneapolis: Fortress Press, 2000), 106–7.

5. 1 John 4:7-12, 19-21.

6. Genesis 12:2.

7. Gary Nelson, *Borderland Churches: A Congregation's Introduction to Missional Living* (St. Louis: Chalice, 2008), 55.

8. 2 Corinthians 9:8 NRSV.

9. Nelson, *Borderland Churches*, 57.

10. Bob Farr, *Renovate or Die: Ten Ways to Focus Your Church on Mission* (Nashville: Abingdon, 2011), 61.

11. David K. Switzer, *Pastoral Care Emergencies* (Minneapolis: Fortress Press, 2000).

12. David Augsburger, *Dissident Discipleship: A Spirituality of Self-Surrender, Love of God and Love of Neighbor* (Grand Rapids: Brazos, 2006), 75.

13. *Sundays and Seasons, Communion Prayer for the Third Sunday in Advent* (Minneapolis: Augsburg Fortress, 2014).

6

A Congregational Approach to Community Organizing

Take away the noise of your songs; I will not listen to the melody of your harps. But let justice roll down like waters, and righteousness like an everflowing stream. (Amos 5:23-24)

Hilltop was an area in North Tacoma, Washington that had become known for the violence of gang wars that occurred there. Murders were as common as rain in the Northwest, with almost daily knifings and drive-by shootings. Not one person felt safe in that neighborhood.

Then something happened that transformed this primarily African American neighborhood into a place of peace and hope. Community organizers worked with area churches and city officials to try and make a difference. A pastor of a congregation in Hilltop who also considered himself chaplain to the larger community had an idea. He had been working for racial harmony and an end to violence in his neighborhood. He and his congregation approached this new coalition with a simple suggestion.

Why not have a very public worship rite at the site of each murder to reclaim that place and bring healing to the family of the victims? The coalition agreed and contacted the local news media about the planned *action. This self-appointed neighborhood chaplain invited the campus pastors from nearby Pacific Lutheran University and leaders of several faith traditions to join him in this cause.*

Every time a murder occurred, this group would show up the following day to acknowledge the tragedy and conduct a cleansing ritual. They always invited members of the community and the victim's family to be present as songs were sung, various religious readings recited, and a liturgy of resurrection was proclaimed. And each time the local news media reported it on television and in the local newspaper.

It was not this act alone that brought peace to a troubled area. But because of it, people there were emboldened to come forward with information that helped law enforcement catch the perpetrators and "clean up" the community. In addition, city officials were encouraged to provide new low-income housing and spruce up the city parks in that neighborhood. Parents no longer kept their children behind locked doors and closed windows. They were able to reclaim their community and live there with a new sense of peace and hope.

This is an example of what good things can happen when people band together around a common cause. It shows what one congregation in partnership with others can accomplish. By the way, the name of the congregation in the Hilltop area is Peace Lutheran Church.

No congregation alone can bear the responsibility for changing their neighborhood or transforming their community. Congregations that are serious about taking the gospel out into the world need to consider the concept of community organizing, which includes partnering with others if they hope to make a difference. As we have suggested, the church is also called to partner with God in God's mission for the sake of the world. This means taking a stand for the biblical imperatives of love, peace, equality, and social justice in their own communities.

Peace Lutheran Church illustrates what Elaine Ramshaw calls *ritual as a force for justice*. It underscores the importance of ritual as suggested in the previous chapter. She writes in her book *Ritual and Pastoral Care*: "Healthy ritual can be a force for social justice in the institutional church and in the world the church serves. The fundamental argument remains the same: the more we know about important human needs, and the more we learn about how ritual can meet or frustrate those needs, the better we can design our liturgy to proclaim and embody the goodness of God's Reign—a reign of justice as well as love."[1]

Healing and transformation occur as congregations address issues that are important to the larger community and as they bring people together to have conversation and to strategize about how to respond to various concerns. "As churches . . . become leaders in public conversations on behalf of a town, village, or community, pastoral care benefits not simply those who attend the church, but the community as a whole."[2] Again, as illustrated by the story of the Hilltop congregation, pastoral care is more than providing comfort for the afflicted—such as those in the neighborhood affected by a tragic death—but rather it is for church leaders and their congregations to participate in and help lead public conversations about all the issues that are germane to those events. "Healing and transformative care requires that congregations recognize their role in creating stronger networks for ordinary care."[3]

What is meant by "community organizing"? Why and how should a congregation consider taking this approach as it seeks to be faithful to carrying out God's mission of healing and redemption in their neighborhood and beyond? This chapter is intended to guide congregations through a process of effective community organizing that includes the following seven steps or building blocks:

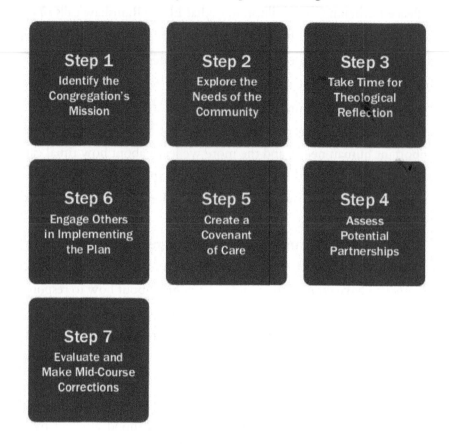

Step 1
Identify the
Congregation's
Mission

Step 2
Explore the
Needs of the
Community

Step 3
Take Time for
Theological
Reflection

Step 6
Engage Others
in Implementing
the Plan

Step 5
Create a
Covenant
of Care

Step 4
Assess
Potential
Partnerships

Step 7
Evaluate and
Make Mid-Course
Corrections

Identifying the Congregation's Mission

One of the questions that is often asked of congregations that are wrestling with their identity and their sense of mission is: *Would this faith community be missed by those in our neighborhood if it ceased to exist?* It is a legitimate question that often causes some serious soul-searching on the part of church leaders and parishioners. Some may make a list of services provided to people in their congregation and local community, such as counseling, holiday food baskets, or quilts for the homeless. While these are important gestures of care, what impact is the congregation really making? How is the Good News of God's love being shared that brings about healing and makes the reign of God more visible in the lives of others?

A congregation would do well to take stock of their sense of purpose, what they value, as well as their context before embarking on a mission of outreach to their neighbors. Is a congregation's ministry focused *inward*, primarily caring for the needs of its own members and exhibiting something of a "country club" mentality? If so, then as long as a congregation offers good worship, education opportunities, and social events for its members, it feels as though it is fulfilling its role or purpose. On the other hand, is a congregation also concerned about what is happening in its context, the neighborhood around it? A congregation that also focuses *outward* and mobilizes its resources to meet the needs of others beyond the church walls understands that their role is not just to serve themselves but to offer their gifts, including the gospel, *for the sake of the world*.

This *tale of two congregations* helps to illustrate the inward and outward distinction. A young pastor was called by a century-old congregation in Brooklyn, New York to serve there in his first call. It had once been a thriving Scandinavian church with a large and beautiful sanctuary. Over the years the neighborhood had changed as African Americans and those of Puerto Rican descent moved in. In fact, most of the current members now lived outside the neighborhood and commuted several miles to church. The young pastor suggested to the parish leadership that if the church was to survive amidst dwindling membership—many of the longtime members were dying off—they would need to reach out to their immediate neighbors by offering some significant ministry and welcoming them to worship. The response of the leadership was "we'd rather die than reach out to our neighbors." The pastor realized that his role was that of a chaplain or even an undertaker who would help them close their doors.

That same pastor was then called to a healthy multi-ethnic church in the Los Angeles area. By contrast to his previous parish in Brooklyn, this congregation had recognized that they needed to shift their focus from inward to outward. Situated in a rapidly changing neighborhood, the congregation chose to intentionally reach out to help meet the needs of the community around them by providing such services as a food and clothing bank, job counseling, and after-school care and tutoring for underprivileged children. They also chose to model their worship after the various ethnic groups in their community and now include hymns, prayers, and scripture readings that are offered in various languages that reflect their neighborhood.

An important question for every congregation to contemplate is not *Why did God originally place us here in this community?* but rather *What is God's missional purpose for us today?* We believe God desires that every congregation share the gospel message in concrete ways in order to meet the real needs of people outside the walls of the church. As such, a congregation that is faithful to this calling needs to explore what are the real and felt needs of the community around them.

The Evangelical Lutheran Church in America has developed a program for congregations called Area Mission Strategies, which includes three goals: 1) Rejuvenate the faith of people who participate in ways that enhance their awareness of God's work and their vocation; 2) Renew the ministry of partner congregations and the members who participate in them; and 3) Call ministries into partnership to have a collective impact on a specific area (such as neighborhood, city, county, etc.). The desired impact on both congregation and community is summarized as follows: "As ministries re-root in their neighborhood, strangers become neighbors and neighbors become friends. Individual lives are transformed through new relationships and new understandings, and the congregations renew their worship and ministry, examining, adapting, and sometimes ceasing established practices to make space for the ever-changing body of Christ."[4]

A congregation that chooses to participate in God's mission in the world can find itself renewed and its community transformed. The process to understanding God's mission for your community today involves three great listenings: 1) To God, 2) to your community of faith, and 3) to your neighbors and the broader community. It begins with listening. "Listening with other potential partners to what God is up to in your area and the work God is calling you to join. Listening within the community of faith for the yearnings of God's people. Listening to God's voice beyond the boundaries of your ministry to hear how God is active and alive in the broader community."[5]

Exploring the Needs of the Community

Listening to those outside the congregation is critical if care is to be offered in a meaningful and appropriate way to one's neighbors. "Caring requires the kind of listening and attending that begins with the simple desire to enter into relationship that honors a primary need of all human beings—to know and be known by other human beings. Before the desire to change must come the desire to connect, and that connection requires efforts at understanding the world from the other's perspective."[6]

Often a congregation thinks it knows what is needed in a given community context. However, it is important to listen to the other's point of view, to get their perspective on what the real and felt needs are in the surrounding area. One method used effectively by congregations and community service agencies is the idea of listening posts. This can take place in one of two ways: a) a congregation might invite community leaders to join them for a neighborhood forum at which time those leaders would share their ideas and concerns with members of a local church, or b) the congregation may choose to send people out into the community to meet with the leaders of various organizations such as the local school, Boys and Girls Club, a church community service agency, and members of the local city government. Below are some suggested questions that could be used.

1. How long have you lived and/or worked in this neighborhood? In that time, have you become aware of our congregation and have knowledge of any of our ministries?
2. How do you understand your particular position or role in relation to the larger community?
3. Have you had an opportunity to meet with other community leaders to share concerns and to strategize about how to meet the needs of people in our area?
4. What do you consider to be among the top five to ten needs or concerns of people in the larger community? Who are the people at risk?
5. What role might our congregation play in helping to meet those needs?
6. What are some creative partnerships we might consider as we seek to provide care for those in our community?
7. Are there resources (such as grants, donors, or volunteers) that we should be aware of that could assist us in planning and carrying out a community mission action plan?

The task of listening does not end with hearing from community leaders, however. The church would do well to listen also to the voices of those who are marginalized or who have less power. For example, in addition to listening to a staff member at the local Boys and Girls Club, why not gather some of the youth together to hear of their concerns, especially related to issues such as school bullying, drugs and alcohol use, sexual abuse, and the like. If a congregation is host to a local Alcoholic Anonymous group, it may be valuable to have conversation with some of the attendees and their sponsors. It is only in hearing from many different voices that a congregation might determine what is good for the community. See Hoeft, Jung, and Marshall's chapter on "Care Engaging Community."[7]

Dennis Jacobson suggests that the "interview"—a conversation with another person—is the primary tool of organizing for mission. In his book *Doing Justice: Congregations and Community Organizing* he writes, "It is a conversation in which we come to understand what is important to another person, what motivates him or her, what is his or her passion. . . . Without being intrusive, the interviewer needs to take the risk of probing to discover the motivational depths of the other person. It means listening for areas of tragedy, pain, anger, passion, and injustice in the other person's life story. . . . The one-on-one interview is a simple, relational tool. A healthy and vital congregation-based community organization cannot be built without it."[8]

Taking Time for Theological Reflection

Another good question for congregations to ask is, *What is God already up to in our neighborhood and how might we participate in this activity?* God is often at work long before a community of faith discovers what its mission needs to be and how to go about helping its neighbors in need. Theological reflection is the art of thinking about God's activity in the world, that is, looking through a theological lens at what is going on in people's lives. As parish leaders seek to assess their community and determine what some of the concerns and needs are that might be addressed, they need to consider what the theological underpinnings of their assumptions are. How does their faith and their understanding of God affect how they might approach a particular problem or issue? For example, one given denomination may lift up the leadership of women in the community and even ordain women as pastors, while another denomination views women as having a lesser role.

Carrie Doehring suggests that people in crisis raise questions and make laments such as "Why is this happening to me?" The answers, she believes, come out of the theological presuppositions that shape their lives and practices. She writes:

> People become most aware of their values when they reach turning points in their lives and must make choices or when they are thrust into decision making because of a crisis. Prior to such moments, they may not have thought much about the values that orient them to the meaning and purpose of their lives. At its simplest, theology is a way to talk about people's deepest values.
>
> The use of theology is what makes pastoral care distinct from other forms of care. . . . Caregivers can assess theologically how people put into practice the values that form their religious orientation by asking questions like these: Do their religious faith and practices give people new life, or exacerbate already painful circumstances? To what extent do people experience the fullness and complexity of God's presence with them?[9]

St. Gregory of Nyssa, an Episcopal congregation in San Francisco, operates with the theological understanding that God loves and welcomes everybody. This congregation exudes hospitality to the point of providing volunteers who in a rainstorm will accompany worshipers with a large umbrella to a cab or personal vehicle. And as one might imagine, this is an inclusive church where people from all walks of life—various ethnic backgrounds, different sexual orientations, and economic situations of all kinds—feel welcome.

There may be differences of opinion within and among religious groups about what would be an appropriate response to a particular social issue. One's image of God will often dictate how an individual or congregation may choose to approach a given concern. When applying theological reflection to a particular situation or need in one's community and deciding on an appropriate action, it is not enough to ask *What would Jesus do?* but more importantly, *Where is God at work and how am I being called to join in that work?*

There are also times when a response to a crisis requires that religious groups transcend their differences and find a way to work together. Such was the case when a major hurricane hit the Florida coast a few years ago, leaving destruction in its wake. The population in a particular coastal town was without access to electricity and clean water for over a week. Many had lost their homes and most businesses were shuttered. The churches of that town—representing different denominations with varied religious views—did agree on one important issue. It was the *Matthew 25 Principle* about clothing the naked, feeding the hungry, and providing shelter for the stranger.[10] Together they mobilized to help a community in crisis by opening their doors as temporary shelters and providing meals. This later led to greater cooperative efforts in that same community among a diverse religious population, resulting, for example, in a Community Food and Clothing Bank sponsored jointly by the area congregations as they sought to care for neighbors in need.

Theological reflection can lead faith communities to envision the world not as it is but as God intends for it to be. To ask the question, "What is God's perfect and promised future for us and our world?," Dennis Jacobson imagines what the world could and should be like under the reign of God. "The world as it should be is rooted in truth, love, and community. In the world as it should be, the voice of conscience is heard. In the world as it should be, people act according to the values of their faith. In the world as it should be, fairness and mutuality reign. The world as it should be is God's dream engaging the nightmare that the world has become."[11]

Assessing Potential Partnerships

It is important that congregations who seek to connect with their community in a vital way seek out healthy partners that have a common sense of mission and like-minded passion of making a difference for good. We are reminded that "Dom Helder Camara, Brazilian Archbishop and champion of the poor, once said: 'If I dream alone, it is only a dream. If we dream together, it is the beginning of reality.' And so it is with the formation of congregation-based community organizations."[12] If a congregation wishes to make an impact on their community they must find others who will share their vision of what could be.

God's mission, as carried out by a congregation and its partner organizations, is to help heal and redeem the world beginning with the local neighborhood. This can be most effectively carried out by means of congregation-based community organizing. "The local congregation is the building block of the organization. Organizing must be linked to the faith and values of the local congregation [and its partners], to its self-interest, to its needs for leadership training, to the realities of its neighborhood . . ."[13]

The exercise of deep listening by a congregation as described earlier in this chapter will hopefully reveal some of the more willing partners in this effort to develop an organization that has power and resources to make a difference in the lives of others. Identifying potential partners begins with who people in the congregation may know, and in this phase, it is good to consider which other congregations and ecumenical groups may be interested in listening with you to the needs of the larger community. Other partners may include social service agencies, local schools, the YMCA and YWCA, a Boys and Girls Club, as well as institutions of higher learning.

As the conversation becomes more serious with potential partners, a network begins to develop that has promise. The conversation includes a discussion of those issues that need to be addressed, focusing perhaps on the top five that may need further research. This network of partners works in a collaborative way, each having an equal say in how to proceed and what issues to tackle. Together decisions are made regarding development of a strategy, funding options, training of volunteers, and the like. Finally, there needs to be a clear understanding among members of this community network on what are the key issues that need to be addressed and where God is wanting transformation to happen. All of this work will be enhanced if it is embedded in prayer and the reading of Scriptures.[14]

Creating an Action Plan and Covenant of Care

Creating an action plan for a congregation-based community organization is more than a simple blueprint of activity. For the network of partners seeking to make a difference in people's lives, it is a covenant of care. It is a way for the congregation in partnership with others to bring its resources of care to meet the needs of those outside church walls. Following Martin Luther's admonition, it is a way of being a "little Christ to the neighbor."[15] Members of the network covenant together for a common purpose and like-minded mission as they seek to bring healing and wholeness to the larger community.

This covenant of care begins with a threefold goal as illustrated in this chapter's opening story. The first is the building of trust among the neighbors one seeks to help. It is important that they understand that the network is not trying to impose its will but rather to work alongside others in the neighborhood who desire to make it a safer and better place. It is important to include valued and recognized leaders in the neighborhood in the creation of an action plan.

The second is to connect with people in the neighborhood—learning from them their joys, their sorrows, their hopes, and their dreams. It is all about establishing relationships and building on the network of care represented by the congregation and its partners.

The third is to form a plan of care that will help people move forward with their lives in hope, no matter what crisis or issue they may be struggling with. Such a network of care would do well to adopt the vision statement of Trinity Lutheran Church in Lynnwood, Washington as they rebuilt following an arson fire: "Healing Hurts, Renewing Hope, and Rebuilding Dreams."

There are some simple steps in developing an action plan or covenant of care listed below.

1. Establish a leadership team and decide on the means of communication among members of the network.

2. Do a final assessment of the neighborhood and perceived needs. This is best done in consultation between the network and members of the neighborhood.

3. Determine what are the top five priorities that might be addressed and decide where to commit the resources of the network.

4. Assess the resources of the network, especially in terms of volunteers and funding. Make a determination of what more will be needed to carry out the plan effectively.

5. Build a budget and seek outside funding if available.

6. Promote the plan among members of the network and recruit volunteers.

7. Provide training for volunteers that will be specific to their assignments.
8. Carry out the plan.
9. Keep the neighborhood informed as to what the network is up to and why.
10. Evaluate the progress and make any mid-course corrections that may be needed.

Engaging Others to Make a Difference

First Evangelical Lutheran is a congregation in Mesa, Arizona that found itself in the midst of a changing neighborhood. As they assessed the demographics and talked with community leaders, they discovered that the population was now largely Latino. They began working with various community agencies to map out a strategic mission plan for reaching out to their neighbors. They called a Hispanic pastor to join their church staff and to work alongside their lead pastor; and they added a Spanish-language worship service.

Because the congregation's membership was now a fraction of what it once had been, many Sunday school rooms sat empty. So the congregation decided to repurpose them for community use. They started a bilingual daycare and preschool program for neighborhood children. A number of community services such as a food bank, health clinic, and a job search program were now located at the church, drawing people in from the surrounding neighborhood.

One challenge remained. The parish leaders asked the question: "How do we inform the members of the congregation and the larger community about all the good ministry that is being offered?" The pastors suggested they create a video highlighting this transition to becoming a neighborhood worship and community center. It was shown to members and prospective members and made available to various community groups. The result was a surge in volunteers who wanted both to help in some tangible way and to affirm this new direction for mission.

This is an example of what it takes to engage others to join in making a difference in the local community. It is not enough to put a plan into action. It is just as important to communicate what is being done and why, as well as to share some of the positive results of those activities.

The implicit goal of community organization is to empower others to make a difference. Sometimes it means engaging the current power structure to do so. It is in organizing people and money to build a network of care that can bring about justice and hope in the public arena. One such organization known for doing this effectively is Habitat for Humanity. It has assembled a network of congregations, community service organizations, and corporate sponsors for the purpose of building affordable housing for those who would otherwise have no home. Many have caught the vision of what this can mean to a community and become engaged in making this dream into a reality.

Evaluating the Work and Making Corrections as Necessary

Once an action plan is in place and people have been mobilized to carry out this *covenant of care* for the sake of the community, God's transformative mission is enhanced as recipients of care experience healing and hope. One important task remains: "to empower the persons, families and community to see themselves as agents of hope and transformation. This requires a realistic assessment of where power lies, how power is operating, and in what ways the people at this table have the capacity for effecting change in a direction that they believe will move toward God's vision for life on earth."[16] There is a popular quote from Mahatma Gandhi: "Be the change you wish to see in the world." Just so, the network of care that is seeking to meet particular needs and bring positive change to a given neighborhood can empower members of that community to become agents of change themselves.

The work of transformation and healing is only just beginning. The congregation-based community action network will need to constantly evaluate what change is taking place and how effective the efforts are in providing a new vision of care for the larger community. Some helpful questions to ponder are as follows. Are people experiencing God's love and grace in the actions of the caregivers? How are people being healed and their lives changed for the good? What unexpected obstacles have arisen that make the delivery of care more difficult than originally thought? Have circumstances changed that require a different approach?

Mid-course corrections are important to consider as an action plan is in process. The vision for healing and transformation may not change, but the objectives and means for achieving it may need to. The action plan should never be cast in concrete, but be a living document that can change and be adapted as necessary. New information may come to light that may change the direction of the plan or at least require a detour. It's like planning a road trip across country. One never knows when a bridge that is out or a road deemed unpassable may require the driver to seek a different route. So it is with a covenant of care that a network has designed for their work together in the community.

The Bible tells us that "where there is no vision, the people perish."[17] There is another truth as well: "Without organization, the vision perishes. Vision without organization is fanciful. Organization without vision is moribund. To become realized, a vision must be organized. To remain dynamic, an organization must be visionary. Congregation-based community organizing needs both vision bearers and organization builders. It is not enough to forge a vision. An organization must be created that can embody and engender that vision."[18]

The vision of a congregation-based community action network is always to partner in God's mission for the healing and transformation of the world. It is a means by which the resources of care in a given congregation as well as its partner organizations can be shared in a meaningful and effective manner to meet the real and felt needs of the larger community. The network provides the organization needed to carry out God's work of care in the world.

Questions for Reflection:

1. What are the three key listenings that will help a congregation determine the needs in a given community and how it might be able to respond?
2. Explain how a congregation-based community organization can be an effective way of delivering care.
3. What are some important considerations when exploring potential partners?
4. How is an action plan like a covenant of care? List the three goals of such a covenant.
5. How are vision and organization inseparably connected when developing a network of care?

Notes

1. Elaine Ramshaw, *Ritual and Pastoral Care* (Philadelphia: Fortress Press, 1987), 88.
2. Jeanne Hoeft, L. Shannon Jung, and Joretta Marshall, *Practicing Care in Rural Congregations and Communities* (Minneapolis: Fortress Press, 2013), 59.

3. Hoeft, Jung, and Marshall, *Practicing Care in Rural Congregations and Communities*, 55.

4. Dave Daubert and Amy Walter-Peterson, *Building Healthy Communities Together: A Framework for Area Ministry Strategy in the Evangelical Lutheran Church in America* (Chicago: Evangelical Lutheran Church in America, 2014), 2.

5. Ibid., 9.

6. Hoeft, Jung, and Marshall, *Practicing Care in Rural Congregations and Communities*, 32.

7. Ibid., 63.

8. Dennis Jacobson, *Doing Justice: Congregations and Community Organizing* (Minneapolis: Fortress Press, 2001), 60.

9. Carrie Doehring, *The Practice of Pastoral Care: A Postmodern Approach* (Louisville: Westminster John Knox, 2006), 111.

10. Matthew 25:31-46 NRSV.

11. Jacobson, *Doing Justice*, 8.

12. Ibid., 27.

13. Ibid., 27 and 39.

14. Daubert and Walter-Peterson, *Building Healthy Communities Together*, 11–13.

15. Martin Luther.

16. Hoeft, Jung, and Marshall, *Practicing Care in Rural Congregations and Communities*, 42.

17. Proverbs 29:18 NRSV.

18. Jacobson, *Doing Justice*, 81.

7

When Prayer is Not Enough: The Power of Ritual to Heal

Rejoice with those who rejoice, weep with those who weep. (Romans 12:15)

It was early Sunday morning when the phone in my hotel room rang. I was serving as chaplain for a Lutheran Marriage Encounter weekend. It was intended to be an enrichment experience for couples that included talks by team members and assignments that the couples would do together in the privacy of their own room, such as sharing their answers to a particular discussion question. We encouraged the couples to be open with each other and answer with complete honesty in order for their relationship to deepen and to grow.

The person on the other end of the line was a pastor who had come to the event at the encouragement of his wife. From our brief interaction during free time, they seemed like a nice, devoted couple. Even though it was five in the morning, the husband was insistent that I come to their room immediately. I sensed the urgency in his voice, so without further explanation I agreed and headed downstairs to their room. I wondered what sort of crisis I might be expected to navigate.

The man met me at the door and ushered me into the room. His wife sat on the bed, her legs in a yoga position. From the red splotches on her face, it was obvious that she had been crying. She looked up at me defiantly, as if to challenge me to "fix" whatever the problem between them was. Her husband motioned me to the lone chair in the room and then sat on the bed next to his wife. He began to explain why they had felt it necessary to see me at such an early hour.

"We've been up all night talking," he explained. "The talk by one of the team couples last night really got to us. Especially when they mentioned how keeping secrets from each other can erode trust and damage a relationship." He paused, as if not sure whether to continue. The woman next to him urged him on with a shove on his shoulder, as if to say "you started this, now finish it."

"So I decided to come clean. I told Carolyn here that I have been having an affair with the parish secretary." At that moment I could see tears welling up in the woman's eyes and my own heart started pounding faster. I thought to myself that I had really stepped into a hornets' nest and wasn't sure how to respond. There was an awkward silence in the room.

Finally I responded, "So how long has this been going on?"

"For about two months."

"Two months too long," Carolyn chimed in.

"I told her it was over and said I realized it was a big mistake."

"So, Carolyn," I interjected, "tell me what you are thinking or feeling at this time."

Carolyn pondered for a moment and said, "I want to believe him. I really do. I don't want this marriage to end. But I'm not sure I'm ready to forgive him yet."

"That may take some time," I replied. "I would encourage you to see a marriage counselor together and see if you can find some reconciliation in order to continue your life together."

We talked for a while longer and then as the conversation seemed to be winding down, the husband asked me: "Could you do something for us? I mean right now, offer a prayer and I don't know what else that could bring us some healing and some peace."

So I prayed with them, offering up the most pastoral prayer I could muster. I asked God for healing and comfort, and that they would be shown the way to restore their marriage. I thought I had covered all the bases. But just as soon as I said "Amen," the husband commented: "Well pastor, you sure do know how to pray, but I guess I expected something more. Like a ritual of some kind."

I left their hotel room feeling like I had failed them. I may have had the right words for a prayer, but it wasn't enough. They had needed something more.

The illustration above is an example of our search for meaning in times of distress. While prayer can offer some comfort and assurance, the power of ritual cannot be underestimated in certain circumstances, especially when one feels as though their world has fallen apart. Elaine Ramshaw suggests in her book *Ritual and Pastoral Care* that "the need for the ritual expression and reinforcement of the symbolic world view is intensified in situations which threaten meaning or coherence . . . [and we] often turn to ritual in times of transition or tragedy. The taken-for-granted everyday world is disrupted, one's place in the social structure is shifted, a relationship one has depended upon for continuity is ended, or undeserved suffering strikes at one's assumptions about God's justice."[1]

Ritual is important in meeting both the needs of individuals and the needs of the community. As we will see in this chapter, ritual can bring healing and restore meaning to those who are struggling to find their way through life's difficult situations. We will explore why an integration of ritual and pastoral care is critical for the church's work today. We will seek to define ritual and determine its purpose in the life of individuals and in the corporate life of the church. We will see the importance of helping people connect with the larger narrative of God's story and why the use of symbol and metaphor is so important. Finally, we will assist the reader in how to assess the need for ritual and how to structure ritual with an appropriate use of resources.

The Definition and Purpose of Ritual

What do the terms "worship," "liturgy," "rites," and "ritual" all have in common? And how are they different? In some faith traditions, worship and liturgy are synonymous, implying a worship structure that is repetitious and much the same from week to week. For example, in many Christian churches, the pastor will often begin worship with the words "Peace be with you" and the congregation will respond "And also with you." The service is composed each week with the same format of prayers, scripture, songs, creeds, and often a celebration of the Eucharist. For those who find themselves just going through the motions, worship may seem as though it were simply ritualistic. For others, this kind of ritual has the power to connect them with the Holy and lift their spirits to new heights.

Ritual is more than religious worship, however. Ritual is something that is practiced by all ethnic groups and cultures. "Human beings take rituals seriously because, in a very real sense, they are essential for our survival. We too employ rituals for establishing courtship, organizing the hunt, caring for offspring, and avoiding life-threatening conflicts. . . . They are the basic vehicle for creating and expressing meaning. They are an indispensable medium by which we make our way through life."[2] Ritual is something that helps give the transitions in our life meaning and purpose. And as suggested, ritual can be a powerful force for good or for ill:

> Positively, it can gather the community in a structure strong enough to hold many people, conflicting points of view, and varied emotions together in unity. It can be engaged to empower and heal participants, and to release and redeem them from the stranglehold of emotional, psychological, or spiritual oppression. Life-giving ritual can create unity out of estrangement, support out of isolation, and hope out of fear or despair. But ritual power also can be engaged to oppress persons or manipulate them.[3]

Rites are usually those rituals designed for use by the faith community to assist individuals and congregations observe various circumstances in life. They may be one-time events that address a particular situation or repeated by a congregation as rites of transition or healing for the common good. Baptism is a good example of a rite that does both. This rite of initiation is generally considered the entry point into the kingdom of God and the beginning of one's life of faith. It is celebrated every time an individual (infant, youth, or adult) has water splashed over them in this corporate rite and then is invited to live as a child of God. Some rites may be done once and privately, such as a rite that some traditions call "Commendation of the Dying." This is meant to bring comfort to both the person dying and those loved ones who watch with them.

Some congregations observe a "Remembrance of Baptism" rite several times a year, particularly on "The Baptism of Our Lord Sunday" in January. This reminds the individual and the community of God's great act of love, forgiveness, and salvation offered them in their baptism. It is also a clarion call to live out the promises of their baptism in daily life. When Trinity Lutheran Church in the Greater Seattle area burned to the ground, the congregation gathered at the site of their demolished building for a "Service of Remembrance" on the occasion of de-consecrating the ground to make way for the building of a new worship and community center. The service began with a remembrance of baptism as worship leaders took fir branches dipped in water and sprayed it on the crowd while worshipers sang a baptismal hymn. Members of the congregation were then invited to share their memories of this sacred place that had been destroyed by an arson fire. They shared stories of weddings, baptisms, funerals, and other events that they cherished in their hearts. This rite was the beginning of healing for the congregation and for others in the larger community.

Rituals are needed to help people through times of transition, suffering, and loss in order to make meaning out of a given situation for their lives. I recall a time when a parishioner who was dying from cancer asked me to share the Eucharist with him and his family in the hospital room. For him, this was an important act of rich communion as together we celebrated God's gifts of forgiveness, eternal life, and salvation. Pastors and church leaders should be aware of the importance of these acts in the lives of their people. "Supporting the practice of spiritual care through rites of transition and healing is of crucial importance in the contemporary challenges of the life of the church."[4]

Connecting with God's Story

We need to know that our lives are part of a greater narrative, that we are connected with God's story of redemption. The goal is to connect people's story with God's story. "Rituals are not only necessary personal resources for growth and stability; they are ways that faith communities frame our journeys in God. . . . We are transformed in part because we begin to understand our story as part of a larger, transcendent narrative. God has chosen to coauthor a redemptive story for us and with us in human history, and in so doing has invited us to reshape radically the horizon of all other storytelling and ritual making."[5]

We experienced this truth in the aftermath of an arson fire and the destruction of the Trinity Lutheran Church campus. At the onset as we were going through our initial grief work as a congregation, we talked about death and resurrection; and, as their pastor, I assured them that just as Jesus came forth from his tomb, there would be new life coming out of this tragedy. It was two and a half years before we dedicated a new church facility. We were in a type of exile or wilderness as we worshiped in a borrowed church building, and held weddings and funerals wherever we could find another congregation willing to take us in. So we began to identify with Moses and the children of Israel wandering through the wilderness in the hope of the promised land. We also talked about God's people who had been later exiled to Babylon and how God provided for their return to rebuild Jerusalem and their temple. It gave us comfort and encouragement along the journey to remember and celebrate a God who fulfills the promises made to God's people.

One of the roles of ritual is to help people open themselves to God and what God is doing in their lives. As they can imagine themselves as part of God's redemptive history, it can help them make meaning out of a transition or difficult situation and open them up to a new and hope-filled future. That is one of the tasks of pastoral care: to help others see how God is engaged in the human story and their story in particular. "When we are willing to admit the possibility of God's presence in ordinary human events, we will be more likely to fashion our human narratives—composed of so many such events—in light of that presence. Ordinary life is transformed when we recognize that our stories bear the presence of God."[6]

Christians connect with the redemptive story of Jesus Christ in a profound way. The Christian tradition is based on the paschal mystery of Jesus celebrated in the sacraments. Ritual becomes "a two-way street where God's action and human action meet. . . . In the sacraments especially, the awareness that 'God is doing something here' overwhelms us with grace, the core of the mystery of God's relation to us."[7] Elaine Ramshaw suggests that all worship is a celebration of our common baptism. Liturgy, which literally means "the work of the people," is living out our baptismal identity. It is embracing the vocation of a Christian life that models that of Jesus. She goes on to suggest that the Easter Vigil—the Queen of Feasts—that is celebrated on Holy Saturday "demonstrates the centrality and communality of baptism as no other ritual can for it remembers the death and resurrection of Christ through remembering our common baptism into that mystery. . . . The font is the focus of the whole community, recognized as the community's present entry into the mystery of cross and resurrection. In celebrating the Easter Vigil we know baptism as the core of our Christian identity, individually and corporately alike."[8]

Connecting the human story with the divine is an important task of pastoral care. In the past, a traditional view of pastoral care was one that seemed more concerned about the individual story alone and not about how it connected with God's metanarrative or the larger story of the faith community. Indeed, the first job of pastoral care is to understand the nuances of a particular human experience, then to help people reframe their stories in light of their faith tradition and God's story. This is where ritual can be so powerful, helping people see how they too fit into God's narrative of hope and healing.

The Power of Symbol and Metaphor

Jesus understood the value of symbol and metaphor, which he used effectively in the parables he told to communicate a greater truth about the reign of God. Just so, the use of symbol and metaphor help the individual and faith community face the discordant and painful in life. This was true for Trinity Lutheran Church when the congregation gathered in the parking lot for worship on a Sunday morning while behind them their sanctuary lay in smoking ruins. The scripture that was shared that morning was from Isa. 43:2-3: "When you pass through the waters, I will be with you; and through the rivers, they shall not overwhelm you; when you walk through fire you shall not be burned, and the flame shall not consume you. For I am the Lord your God, the Holy One of Israel, your Savior."[9] These verses filled with metaphor helped the congregation to confront the tragedy in front of them and yet to do so with hope. We salvaged the charred remains of the large cross that had hung above the altar. The following Good Friday we mounted it on the stage of a building we had been renting for worship. It was a critical symbol of what we had been through and how it connected with the passion of Jesus.

The use of symbol and metaphor in ritual is important to meeting people's needs at the deepest level, shedding light on those things that are often so painful to face while helping them discover God at work creating for them a better tomorrow. Susan Marie Smith suggests that "ritual has therapeutic value not only because it attributes symbolic meaning to experience. The repetition of ritual also helps create a sense of continuity in our lives by linking the past to the present and the present to the future. . . . Rituals become a dependable source of security and comfort. . . . They give tangible shape to our hopes and dreams."[10]

Rituals that make use of symbol and metaphor help to express the tradition of a faith community and how it shapes meaning out of the situations of life that people encounter. Elaine Ramshaw explains this eloquently in her book *Ritual and Pastoral Care*:

Formal rituals carry the core meanings of the social group performing them, the meanings which determine that group's world view. They do this through the use of symbols which have many layers of significance and a wide range of interpretation. Through such symbols as a wooden cross or the act of giving bread or the community's forming a circle, we express the deepest meanings we know of . . .

The need for the ritual expression and reinforcement of the symbolic world view is intensified in situations which threaten meaning or coherence. That is why people who go along without access to the tradition's symbols often turn to ritual in times of transition or tragedy.[11]

Throughout the centuries, the Christian church has understood the power of using symbols. A ship hanging in the nave symbolized the church and its journey through the waters of life. The breaking of bread and pouring of wine symbolized—and in some traditions became—the body and blood of Jesus who offered himself on the cross for the salvation of humankind. At Christmas, some churches make use of the Advent wreath whose candles mark the four Sundays in Advent. And of course there is the Christmas tree that adorns sanctuaries and living rooms alike, and whose lights—originally candles—remind us of the light of Christ that came into the world in the form of a baby born at Bethlehem. There are vestments and paraments of various colors for the church year that are adorned with symbols such as a fish, a cross with a crown, and the Greek letters *Chi Rho*, all of which represent Jesus Christ as God's Son and Savior of all.

The careful use of metaphor and symbol can both transport and restore people; they can offer a vision or at least a glimpse into God's intended and promised future. They can change people's lives by giving meaning to their present situation. As Smith suggests, "meaning is made in metaphor and is stored in symbol."[12] Rituals that make good use of metaphor and symbols can become a vehicle for not only making meaning, but also transforming individuals and communities.

Smith talks about the importance of those who are creating rituals to find an *overarching metaphor* that gives meaning and structure to a given rite. "A foundational metaphor has the power to inspire powerful symbolic action and a deep sense of truth."[13] She speaks symbolically of the metaphor being a *bridge* to new life and a renewed sense of purpose. Symbolic action like the sprinkling of water upon the crowd at Trinity's Service of Remembrance was a powerful action that reminded them of the promises God made to them in baptism. It reconnected them with God's story of redemption and enabled them to look beyond themselves and assist other victims of arson in the larger community. They adopted a new motto for their ministry: "Healing Hurts, Restoring Hope, and Rebuilding Dreams." This propelled them into a renewed sense of mission with the conviction that God was calling them to help heal the world, to reach out to those in need of healing in their neighborhood and beyond.

Assessing the Need and Structuring a Ritual

How do we know when there is a need for a rite or ritual, such as in the opening case study of a marriage in trouble? Smith believes that "the answer requires truth telling, honesty, ritual competence, and creativity. In assessing spiritual ritual need, it is important not to be limited by what people ask for nor by what the pastor immediately imagines. Assessing spiritual ritual need requires prayer and being open to the Spirit. It requires deep listening."[14]

Good pastoral care requires careful listening and accurately responding to the story of others. It is important also to listen for the issues beneath the surface. What is the person really feeling and from what well does it spring? "To be understood and accepted by another person is a treasured dimension of human living. It is also the first movement of any kind of care. We listen carefully in order to get another's story straight. We listen attentively to others so that our response connects with their understanding of their story."[15]

One of the first steps in determining the need for ritual is to understand what a person or community is going through, to know the depth of their experience. In the scripture that began this chapter, St. Paul seems to suggest that we must have empathy for others. Empathy means to walk in their shoes and feel what they're feeling, whether it be joy or sorrow. This is where we begin to assess if there is a need for ritual, and if so, what kind of rite might be considered for a given situation.

This is especially important when deciding whether to use an existing rite or create one that may be more appropriate in responding to a particular circumstance. An example of this is when one is asked to provide comfort for someone who is dying, which involves ministering to their loved ones as well. Does one simply use a rite from an Occasional Services Book called "Commendation of the Dying," or perhaps adapt it to the occasion?

For example, a pastor was visiting with a parishioner who was in hospice care at home and with his wife, who had been his caregiver for months. The pastor had made numerous visits to the home and was surprised that the man was still hanging on. After some deep listening to the couple, he realized that the man was ready to die but the wife refused to let him go. What was needed was not just a prayer of solace, but a ritual of letting go that would provide release for both the dying man and his wife. The pastor shared a simple rite and prayed with them, suggesting it was okay for the man to let loose of this life and release himself into the loving arms of God. There were tears shed as the wife acknowledged she had been hanging on too tight and it was time to say goodbye. Within a few hours the man had died a peaceful death; and the wife, while grieving, also felt a sense of relief. When the pastor met with her the next day to begin planning the funeral service, she shared a psalm that had offered her great comfort: "Weeping lingers for the night, but joy comes in the morning."[16]

Smith confirms this process of assessing and planning a ritual as an act of pastoral care:

> The process of planning a Christian ritual begins with one who has the eyes to see that a ritual is needed. . . . It is important to look not only for existing rites, but also for a creative third way. . . . In situations where there is not already a standard rite available, the starting point for competent ritual assessment and creative rite making is compassion, empathy, and deep listening for vulnerability in the feelings and state of the focal person. Ritual assessment is a spiritual practice with a pastoral practical application.[17]

Rituals are important not only for the individuals for whom the rite may be intended, but for the whole faith community as well. While one or more persons may be seeking healing of a difficult situation or commemorating one of life's passages such as a marriage or birth of a child, all those who are present will be affected by their experience of the rite, and in some cases even transformed. Those who create ritual "must be aware that although focused on one or more persons, a Christian ritual is always offered to the glory of God, and thereby touches many persons [even] beyond those present at the rite itself. Rituals are powerful for the very reason that they are bigger than any one person."[18]

The structure of a rite could form a liturgy that includes the following components: scripture, prayer, music, story, and response. One must take into account not only the particular need that is being addressed, whether individual or corporate, but also the congregational culture, the immediate context, and the receptiveness of persons for whom the ritual is intended. Anderson and Foley offer the following guidelines when creating a ritual:

- *Respect the chronological priority of the human story in the shaping of the ritual.* Let the story of crisis or loss, change or transition—the whole story—be heard. . . .

- *Allow a significant role for nonverbal symbols in this ritualizing.* There is a time when words inevitably fail and symbolic gesture becomes necessary. . . .

- *Resist the compulsion to explain such action.* Honor its ambiguity. . . .

- *Attend to the particularity of the moment.* . . .

- *Beware of overcomplicating the ritual.* More is not always better; sometimes less is more.[19]

I recall participating in the "Blessing of the Fishing Fleet" one spring in Alaska. The ritual was very simple and seemed to keep in mind many of the above considerations. The rite began with a remembrance of those who had lost their lives at sea during the previous fishing season. Loved ones gathered near the water and as names were read, an individual in a boat just offshore would toss a floral wreath into the water. When all the names had been read, I offered a prayer of thanksgiving for their lives. The families responded by releasing balloons into the air to commemorate the new life of their loved ones with God. It was a very moving experience for all.

It is important to create a space for ritual to happen, as in the above illustration. And when creating a rite, it is important to consider those things that will help bond the community through story and a common experience. Creating meaning and offering hope are among the goals of ritual worship. An effective ritual involves participation in the rite by all those present, not just the presider. This helps people to identify more deeply with their faith tradition as well as to connect more profoundly with each other and with God.

There are many occasions when the church might consider using a rite or ritual to mark one's journey through life. The following is a list of some of those transitions in life, some that are often observed and others that could be considered:

- For an engagement, marriage, or divorce
- When one loses a job or begins retirement
- At the conception of a child, a birth, an adoption, or a miscarriage
- A time of a serious illness, when one is dying, and one's death and resurrection
- When one goes into the armed services and when one returns from service, especially war
- For times of transition in the lives of young adults, such as graduation and leaving home

Examples of rites for a few of these life transitions listed above can be found in the Appendix.

A Matter of Authenticity

Finally, when considering what kind of ritual may be helpful and appropriate in a given setting, it is good to keep in mind what Gordon Lathrop calls the *permeable boundaries* between various cultures and between faith and culture. "The Christian interest in the discovery of permeable boundaries between cultures is not based only on the general hope for mutual respect and fruitful human exchange. The Christian interest in cultural interpretation arises especially from the deep desire to speak and ritualize the truth about the mercy of God so that this truth may be heard everywhere."[20]

There are times when symbols from a particular culture can add to a Christian ceremony, such as a ritual burning of local grass at the funeral of a Native American believer or the tradition of pouring two colors of sand into a glass container at a wedding to indicate that two people are becoming as one. Such symbols, however, should always point to the greater truth of God's love in Jesus Christ. Ritual care for others in a Christian context needs to be authentic and true to the beliefs of the community of faith that is extending such care.

The calling of the church is about more than just finding more ways to meet the needs of people. "It is a matter of *authenticity*. It is about being clear with the very story and its claims that gave birth to the church and continue to give it its life. It is to bring light to age-old questions: Who are we? In what do we hope? What are we to do, and how shall we live?"[21]

The church is called to make a difference in people's lives and to participate in the healing and transformation of communities. In order to do so, it must be genuine in its care for others and motivated by a desire to love others for the sake of the One who promises new life in Christ. Authentic *ritual care* calls for a bold witness to God's grace. Such a witness can bring about healing and renewal.

Questions for Reflection:

1. How is ritual an act of pastoral care?
2. Why is "deep listening" so important in determining the need for and planning a ritual? Can you think of an example of this?
3. What is meant by connecting our story with God's story? Explain what is meant by a "metanarrative."
4. What are some considerations when deciding if a ritual is needed, and if so what kind of rite might be created that is appropriate to a given situation?
5. When planning a ritual, why should one consider the impact not just on the individual but also on the larger community?

Notes

1. Elaine Ramshaw, *Ritual and Pastoral Care* (Philadelphia: Fortress Press, 1987), 25–26.

2. Herbert Anderson and Edward Foley, *Mighty Stories, Dangerous Rituals: Weaving Together the Human and the Divine* (San Francisco: Jossey-Bass, 1998), 22.

3. Susan Marie Smith, *Caring Liturgies: The Pastoral Power of Christian Ritual* (Minneapolis: Fortress Press, 2012), 3.

4. Ibid., 21.

5. Anderson and Foley, *Mighty Stories, Dangerous Rituals*, x, 37.

6. Ibid., 40.

7. Ramshaw, *Ritual and Pastoral Care*, 35.

8. Ibid., 37.

9. Isaiah 43:2-3 NRSV.

10. Anderson and Foley, *Mighty Stories, Dangerous Rituals*, 49.

11. Ramshaw, *Ritual and Pastoral Care*, 25–26.

12. Smith, *Caring Liturgies*, 87.

13. Ibid., 70.

14. Ibid., 34.

15. Anderson and Foley, *Mighty Stories, Dangerous Rituals*, 45.

16. Psalm 30:5 NRSV.

17. Smith, *Caring Liturgies*, 37.

18. Ibid., 56.

19. Anderson and Foley, *Mighty Stories, Dangerous Rituals*, 130.

20. Gordon W. Lathrop, *Holy People: A Liturgical Ecclesiology* (Minneapolis: Fortress Press, 2006), 166.

21. Rick Barger, *A New and Right Spirit: Creating an Authentic Church in a Consumer Culture* (Herndon, VA: Alban Institute, 2005), 3.

8

Developing a Vision and Strategy for A Discipleship Congregation

For surely I know the plans I have for you, says the Lord, plans for your welfare and not for harm, to give you a future with hope. (Jeremiah 29:11)

The new pastor had only just arrived when some members of the congregation approached him. *"What are you going to do about the PF Chang Marathon, pastor?"* they asked.

"Can you kindly tell me what the problem is?"

"Well, for the past several years now," one of the members responded, *"the route of the race goes right by our church and the police block all the roads that lead to our church except from the north end."*

"It's always the Sunday of Martin Luther King's birthday weekend," added another. *"Attendance at worship and Sunday school go way down because many people can't get to church."*

"That could be a problem," the pastor agreed. *"The race is only a few weeks away and I don't see how we can solve this issue in time for this year. But let me think about it and talk with some folks."*

A few weeks later at a meeting of the church's Outreach Team, the pastor brought up the issue of the marathon. "Let's think outside the box," he said.

"What could we do about this for next year?" The committee sat in silence for a few minutes, pondering the question. Then one member piped up: "They have a water station just down the street from us at the neighborhood park. Maybe we could see if we could take charge of it next year."

The other members agreed it was an idea worth pursuing and a plan was set in motion. One contacted the person in charge of the PF Chang Marathon and was told the church could sponsor the water station the next year. Another member began to round up people to help serve at the station, contacting the Boy Scout troop that met at the church, members of the youth group and parents of the church's preschool, as well as the local neighborhood association. Yet another contacted the local news media.

The following January everything was ready. On its website, PF Chang listed the congregation as one of the sponsors of the water stations, articles appeared in the newspaper, and talk-show hosts on the radio marveled at a congregation stepping forward to join the cause. It was a lot of free publicity. Finally, the church ordered water bottles with the name of the church with its website imprinted on them that would be given away to the runners as they passed by the station.

The night before the race, the congregation hosted a Saturday-night worship service for members of the church, the runners, and marathon volunteers. They dubbed it "A Runners Service," and the sermon focused on running the race of faith. The church was packed. Later, members gathered alongside of the runners and volunteers in the Parish Hall for refreshments. Special T-shirts were gifted to the runners and volunteers at that time as well. The next day the water station served these same people.

The congregation had turned a problem into an outreach opportunity. Because of all the publicity surrounding these events and especially the exposure to the church's hospitality on Saturday night, people in the neighborhood began to inquire about the congregation and many started to attend worship services there. Some neighbors commented that before this, they had driven by the church daily and not paid any attention to it. Now they noticed it and acclaimed its newfound reputation for caring about the larger community around it. Becoming a missional congregation was a major goal coming out of a year-long strategic planning process, and this was one big step in that direction.

How does a congregation turn a vision for mission into reality? It begins with a strategic planning process that focuses on answering the question: *How is God calling us through our ministry in this place to partner with God in the healing and redemption of the world?* Many of the elements needed to answer that critical question will be addressed in this final chapter.

What Is Vision?

Vision is important to the future of a congregation and its community. It involves taking stock of what is and then painting a compelling picture of what could be. "Vision is the beginning point for leading the journey. Vision focuses. Vision inspires. . . . Vision is our alarm clock in the morning, our caffeine in the evening. Vision touches the heart. It becomes the criterion against which all behavior is measured . . . the focus on vision disciplines us to think strategically."[1]

A congregation that has no vision, no sense of where it is going, is likely to stagnate. From our experience, it seems that the average "life span" of a congregation is now less than twenty-five years. This means that if a congregation doesn't reinvent itself and re-envision its future, it is not likely to survive and thrive as a vital, missionary force for change. They say that failing to plan is planning to fail. And so it is with a church that has no vision for the future, no sense of where God is leading it.

Once an individual or organization captures a vision and begins to pursue it, God opens the door of opportunity. Incredible possibilities turn into reality, and often in surprising ways. Such was the case for a pastor in St. Paul, Minnesota who had a dream of feeding the hungry in her community. The following story was reported by the Evangelical Lutheran Church in America in "Living Lutheran," an online newsletter for congregational leaders.

A little more than a year ago, Shobi's Table was just an idea in Margaret's head. As a pastor and social worker, she said, "I had an image of taking church to the street." Margaret [Kelly] remembered thinking, "A good meal would be a way to bring people into church."

Informing her vision was her experience as a case manager at an emergency shelter in Minnesota's Ramsey County. During the three years she worked there, she noticed that the people who came for help had several recurring issues.

People with mental illnesses have serious health issues to cope with related to their medications, including obesity and diabetes. A lack of access to fresh food exacerbates these problems. And while there are food pantries and food "shelves" in the area, these generally do not offer fresh and minimally processed food. . . . Margaret notes a lack of transportation is also a significant barrier for people at the margins . . .

One of the largest green lights flashed on when Margaret approach John Hogenson, lead pastor at St. Andrew's Lutheran Church in Mahtomedi, Minnesota about becoming a congregational partner with Shobi's Table. "He loved our proposal," she said.

He also told her, "I know someone with a food truck." That someone happened to be a member of his congregation who was looking for other organizations to use his truck on days when he wasn't. Then St. Andrew's proceeded to make a grant to purchase food for Shobi's . . .

Ten people show up regularly on Thursday to prepare the meal at Gustavus Adolphus Lutheran Church in St. Paul, which graciously lends their kitchen to Shobi's. The dedicated workers can get there easily, thanks to public transportation.

And once the hand pies and salads are ready, they're off to serve lunch. Among them are Noah, Candy and her daughter and fiancé, and Maurice, a father who brings his one-year-old along. Like Noah, about two-thirds of the group has been homeless and some struggle with mental illness and addictions. Some people are in recovery, and some are working poor, and others are working toward employment.

"They are the evangelists," said Margaret of the group. "I'm there for good order. They walk up and down the block and invite people for a meal. . . ."

This ministry "just keeps opening up for us, which is also very scary," she added. "We've been called into this and given the resources. It seems very big, but we're just serving a meal, saying prayers, and being community together."[2]

Pastor Margaret Kelly was driven by a vision for serving people on the margins by providing food and creating community. Her enthusiasm was contagious and other people caught the vision, eager to help make it a reality. Church leaders likewise must endeavor not just to envision the future but also "to communicate the vision and find ways for others to embrace it. Most people have a difficult time seeing things that aren't already in place. We have to find ways to help them see what we have already seen."[3]

What Is Strategic Planning?

Alan Roxburgh challenges traditional thinking about strategic planning in his book *Missional Map-Making: Skills for Leading in Times of Transition.* He suggests that planning methods based on a traditional strategic-planning process seldom result in changes or preferred outcomes that have been hoped for unless congregations are open to genuine change and transformation.[4] Below is a summary of that process.

Planning usually begins with an internal audit that gathers information concerning the health and vitality of the congregation. Following this phase, an external audit collects data about the neighborhood context in which the congregation is situated. The goal is to create a profile for people living within a five-mile radius that includes such things as age, ethnic and socioeconomic demographics, lifestyle, beliefs, and habits.

The next stage often involves creating or revising a congregational mission statement (or values statement) that takes God's basic purposes and connects them with the information that has been gathered. What results is a description of the congregation's mission, defining its core values and how it lives those out. The following example comes from Desert Streams Church in Surprise, Arizona: "Inviting everyone to a new life in Christ, a deeper relationship with Christ, and Spirit-filled service for Christ."

Developing a vision statement is usually the next step toward creating a new vision for the congregation's mission. It is here that the congregation asks the question, *What is God's preferred and promised future for our ministry?* The vision may include descriptions of what the congregation hopes to achieve and is normally stated in preferred outcomes. It is intended that this statement conveys to both insiders and outsiders *a vision of where the church is going.*

The final stage involves developing a plan with concrete, measurable actions that will help the congregation achieve its vision. This includes bringing all current ministries into alignment with the larger purpose, this new vision for mission. The guiding question here for every area and act of ministry is, *How will what we do help us achieve God's perceived vision in this place?* A timeline is established for the achievement of specific objectives and an evaluation process set in place so that the leadership can periodically assess the progress of the vision plan and make adjustments as necessary.

How does a congregation go about developing a strategic plan and establishing a vision for a new future for their ministry? Keeping in mind the four stages outlined above, there are six simple steps involved that provide a practical guide for the visioning process. They include the following: 1) Assembling a Vision Team, 2) Listening and Learning, 3) Creating a New Vision, 4) Getting Everyone on Board, 5) Financing a Mission Plan, and 6) Evaluating and Updating the Mission.

Assembling a Vision Team

The Vision Team exists for learning, discernment, and establishing guidelines to lead the congregation into a new future. It should be no fewer than five and no more than ten. It should not be made up solely of the elected leadership of the congregation. In fact, it is sufficient to have one member of the church council or vestry serve as a liaison to the rest of the leadership team. In some cases, the congregational president may wish to serve in an ex-officio manner and should always be welcome at meetings of the Vision Team. It is assumed that the pastors of the church will serve along with selected lay members of the congregation. Look for people who are innovative, open to new ideas, respected by their peers, and spiritually sound. It is also good to have a mix of new members along with more established influencers in the parish.

Once a Vision Team has been established, there is some preliminary work to be done as they begin a process of discernment. Below is a worksheet that offers a suggested overview of their task.

CREATING A VISION FOR MISSION: THE PROCESS

1. *Missio Dei:* How do we become partners in God's mission?
2. Making Mission Personal: How do we live that out faithfully and effectively?
3. Goal is to develop a *Vision for Mission* for (name of congregation).
4. Identify and articulate core values.
5. Assessment Part 1: What are the assets, resources, gifts of the congregation?
6. Assessment Part 2: What are the felt needs in the community? Where do the two meet?
7. Consider the strategy of "Grow, Hold, and Fold." (What new things might we consider? What do we need to keep doing and perhaps do better? What are those things we can celebrate and discontinue?)
8. Create a process for developing broad ownership in the congregation.
9. Develop a "Vision for Mission" that becomes a roadmap or template for the staff and leadership; set short-term priorities along with longer term missional objectives.
10. Plan for ongoing evaluation of the mission—keeping the **focus on the vision** and fine-tuning the missional objectives to move the vision forward.

The Vision Team in consultation with the pastor and church leadership needs to determine what kind of a congregation they are and aspire to be. Anthony Robinson, in his book *Changing the Conversation: A Third Way for Congregations*, suggests that there are at least three kinds of congregations. There is the *open-set* congregation, where anyone can say or think whatever they want. There is the *bounded-set* congregation, which has very clear and bold boundaries and beliefs, often with little room for difference of opinions. Then there is the *centered-set* congregation, which has a clear center of purpose and belief but is open to questioning and also values differences among its members. Robinson calls this the "third way" and explains:

> In the centered set the task of the congregation, or its leaders, is not so much to police the boundaries as it is to define and articulate its center. "This is who we are and what we are about. You decide if it's right for you." This is the message of the centered-set [purpose-driven] congregation. . . . Many congregations will find the centered-set concept helpful in a world in which extremes of open and bounded sets are both common, and each in their way inadequate.[5]

Vision is made up of the path God is calling a congregation to take in order to fulfill its purpose. For Tony Robinson, vision and purpose are necessarily connected. As members of the congregation ask "Where are we headed?" and "Tell us where we are going," they are really asking "What is our purpose?" It is not difficult for the Vision Team to come up with interesting and compelling new ideas. "What is difficult, but crucially important, is being fairly clear about our purpose and staying on purpose. Another way to put this is to say that vision must be 'strategic,' which means that vision is related to purpose, that vision advances purpose."[6]

Church leaders sometimes make a huge assumption; they believe that where God's Spirit is leading, the members will want to follow. This is not always true, of course. Some members will be eager to jump on board. Some will drag their heels but eventually come around. And still others will stubbornly resist any change, as was illustrated in chapter three.

It is not always easy for a congregation to embrace a missional vision that invites everyone to join in a common purpose: *that of extending God's reign of peace, justice, love, and healing to the world around them.* To help the congregation move forward, the task of the vision team is threefold: first, to discern God's vision for the congregation through prayer and careful listening to others; second, to find concrete ways to make that vision a reality; and third, to clearly communicate the vision and how everyone has a stake in moving the congregation from point A to point B.

Listening and Learning

One of the most important tasks of the Vision Team and church leadership is to pay attention to what God is up to in their context and how this connects with the congregation and larger community.

This requires both listening and learning. In chapter seven we explored how to go about this work and the three kinds of listening that are crucial: a) listening to God, b) listening to the congregation, and c) listening to the needs expressed by the neighbors and wider world. Listening can be personal, such as a one-on-one conversation; but listening can also be more communal in nature, gathering people together for a rich dialogue and exchange of ideas.

The goal of listening is to learn from what has been heard and how this might both inform the congregation's present ministry and shape its future. Intentional listening builds trust and openness in the life of the faith community. "Listening cultivates healthy diversity within congregational life and affirms its presence as a shared core value. If diversity is unappreciated, threatening dysfunction, needless conflict and relationship tensions ensue. When listening refines community, life in community is less threatening. Opinions are welcomed. Visions become larger because they are a shared reality."[7]

Congregations are called to be incarnational communities that clearly live out the gospel together. "We must discover and imagine what it means to be church in the particular neighborhood and context to which we have been called. This requires being organic instead of institutional, and emphasizing people rather than places, community rather than meetings, movements on a mission rather that building of a membership. The church is better understood as a people, a community, a way of life."[8] This discovery begins by listening and learning from others and from God.

Creating a New Vision

Someone once said that a *vision without a plan is only a dream, and a plan of action without vision is only a longer list of things to do.* This is the critical task of the Vision Team, to craft a new vision for the congregation and put some legs on it by creating a mission plan inspired by this vision that will help the congregation live into God's preferred and promised future.

Skilled church leaders are able to help a congregation envision a new future, to consider what could be. The Vision Team is able to take the information they have gathered and begin to reframe and refocus the mission of the congregation that is more in line with their present reality and also faithful to where they perceive God is leading them to serve. Creating a new vision is never easy but it is essential to a healthy and vital future for Christ's church in every time and place.

Congregations often ignore the reality around them, are content with living in the past, and blind to the mission God is calling them to in the present day. They often listen to only what they want to hear and have their minds made up about what and how church should be. This is why it is so important for church leaders to invite people in the congregation and community into a conversation about what could be.

The visioning process is an exercise in spiritual discernment as church leaders try to determine God's preferred and promised future for their congregation. Pat Keifert suggests that such discernment involves a fourfold task of a) *discovering*, b) *experimenting*, c) *visioning for embodiment*, and d) *learning and growing*. The vision team sets out to discover what God is up to in their midst by viewing opportunities for care through the lens of the gospel. While yet in the visioning process, church leaders may experiment with new ideas sparked by their imagination of ways that the congregation could carry out its mission of caring for others. The Vision Team seeks to embody God's love and grace in a practical manner with concrete plans. And throughout the process, the Vision Team along with congregational members are continuing to learn and grow in their understanding of where God is leading them. All of this requires open communication and opportunities for many to share their input.

Getting Everyone on Board

Consider holding a leadership retreat where all the church staff and church leaders gather together for a brainstorming session. Make sure that all ministry leaders are invited to attend, including the leader of the Altar Guild and coordinators for women's and men's ministries as well as others in key ministry roles. Youth leaders should be included as well to give their perspective. This activity will go a long way in building broad ownership for a new vision for mission.

Take time to list potential areas of ministry that could be part of a new vision. Include both present ministries and future opportunities. The Vision Team can share some of their key learnings from listening to various groups and individuals that can inform how to frame this potential list for the mission plan. Then ask people to gather at tables designated with a specific area of ministry such as youth or community outreach. A scribe is selected by the group to write down a summary of their group conversation to share later with the larger group. The table conversation is guided by the following questions:

1. What are the strengths, assets, and resources that our congregation has to contribute to a new vision for mission?
2. What are the key values that inform our ministry as a congregation (e.g., vibrant worship, a commitment to forming disciples, community outreach, etc.)?
3. What do we know about the felt needs of the community around us, and how can we use our resources to help meet those needs?

4. What are some new opportunities that God seems to be placing before us?
5. Are there any obstacles that might prevent us from addressing these challenges?
6. How does all of this inform our vision of where we need to be going as a church?

The Vision Team then takes the ideas and information shared at the leadership retreat and adopts or creates categories under which to insert missional objectives based on the recommendations of the group. In consultation with the church staff and congregational leaders, judgment is made as to which objectives in each category are priorities. Which of those items are most important and can be tackled in the first year? Smart goals can then be developed for ministries that will help the congregation advance the first-year priorities. (See below.) Congregational leaders can tentatively set the priorities for the second year and the third. This lays out a roadmap for how the mission plan will be implemented.

The Vision for Mission Plan is intended to be a guide for how the congregation will live into its new future. It is a map of how the journey may unfold. The plan is subject to ongoing evaluation—how are we doing and are we doing it well?—and also to adjustments along the way. As described earlier, such planning may be compared to going on a road trip. You map out your travels but for some good reason decide to take a detour. It is okay to tweak and shift priorities along the way.

DESIGNING SMART GOALS
Specific
Measurable
Accountable/Authority
Realistic
Timely

Example: "Design and implement by (date) a new young couple's Bible study group after contacting 10 couples. Select couples in the 20 to 40 something age range."

Does it meet the criteria?

• **Specific:** "Design and implement by (date) a new couple's Bible Study group for couples ..."
• **Measurable:** 10 couples, due date, 20–40 something age range.
• **Accountable/authority:** authority granted by having it as a goal and by allowing staff person in charge to select the people to contact
• **Realistic:** negotiable depending upon due date selected
• **Timely:** a specific date included in the goal, meeting a specific need.

It is important to lift up a vision of what God's preferred and promised future will look like based on the work of the Vision Team in consultation with the church leadership. It is equally essential that the leadership stress the necessity for adopting a new vision and moving the congregation in a new direction. "Skillful leaders nurture a sense of urgency in their congregations. They foster a passionate desire to see the church live out its intended purpose to sing the song [of the gospel] in this new and strange world. This is the crucial difference between congregations that live in their memories and those who live in anticipation of the future."[9]

Financing a Mission Plan

Congregations have an annual operating budget that provides a means for funding various aspects of ministry. It usually covers the salary and benefits for the church staff, the care of buildings and grounds, the support of youth and education programs, and so on. If seen solely as a budget to do its business, members often fight over priorities—of what line items to support. Likewise people are seldom inspired to give generously to a church budget.

What if the leadership replaced the talk about budget and instead presented a "Mission Finance Plan" to the congregation, linking it to the new Vision for Mission. Having a clear sense of purpose can make a difference in encouraging people to support it financially and to share other gifts like their time and talents. It is easier to become passionate about getting behind a financial plan that is intended to help the church effectively carry out its mission.

Darrell Guder believes this reorientation is necessary if a congregation is to be truly missional. He writes: "[T]he main business of many mission committees is to determine how to spend the mission budget rather than view the entire congregational budget as an exercise in mission."[10]

The table below is one way of evaluating the way a congregation funds its ministry.[11]

Internal Focus	External Focus
How much we keep	How much we give away
Church is a holding tank	Church is a pipeline
Scarcity mentality	Abundance mentality (loaves and fishes)
Church savings	Microloans
Giving	Empowering
Pledge drives	Jesus-like generosity
Paying for things	Providing seed money
Giving to the church [congregation]	Giving to the church and other organizations

Once a congregation understands that it is not simply the gathered people of God but also the scattered people of God, the leadership and members begin to understand mission support in a new way. It is not about funding pet projects but rather about funding God's missional imperative: to go into all the world and make disciples.[12]

Evaluating and Updating the Mission

One of the temptations of church leaders is to divert from the plan, especially if there is resistance expressed by church staff or members. This is one of the main reasons that such planning often fails to make a difference. The plan gets shelved or aspects of it are co-opted. It is important to stay the course, and the way leadership responds to those who seek to challenge the vision plan based on their own needs or misconceptions can make all the difference.

This is illustrated by Prince of Peace, a congregation in Phoenix, Arizona, that decided to add a second worship service as an outreach opportunity to meet the needs of young adults and young families in their community. This meant moving the cherished time of the traditional worship service from 9 am to 8:30 am in order to add a service of praise and celebration at 10:30 am, with an education hour in between. A number of older members objected to the change, saying that coming a half-hour earlier was a hardship. They directed their complaint to the church council president, who then explained that the congregation had voted on a vision plan that included adding a second worship service for the purpose of outreach. She said that because they were coming a half-hour earlier, many more people would be able to come and hear the gospel in a more contemporary setting. This explanation seemed satisfy the detractors. The leadership was not dissuaded and continued to move forward with other parts of the mission plan.

One of the ways to effectively move the vision forward and to make sure it is widely embraced and not put on the shelf, is to develop a strategy such as the one below.

CARRYING THE VISION FORWARD: THE ROLE OF THE LEADERSHIP TEAM

COUNCIL AND STAFF: CHAMPIONS OF THE VISION
- Build public support for the vision/strategic plan.
- Help promote the vision through temple talks, newsletter, bulletin updates, website, etc.
- Use the vision as a template for future planning—help people make the connection!

IMPLEMENTATION
- Develop SMART goals for missional objectives for the current year.
- Determine who is responsible and provide necessary support.
- Maintain accountability: e.g. updates on progress in achieving goals.
- Connect the missional objectives with your Mission Spending Plan (budget).

CELEBRATION
- Quarterly team meetings of council and ministry team leaders to assess progress.
- Report at team meetings indicating progress to date offered by council president and lead pastor.
- Celebrate achievements with congregation at worship and congregational meetings, newsletters, blogs, social media.

ONGOING EVALUATION
- Every council meeting should be an opportunity to lift up the Vision for Mission.
- Annual leadership retreat is an opportunity to review and fine-tune missional goals for the coming year.
- Each year establish a new set of priorities along with continuing plans for ministry.

Church staff and congregational leaders are critical to the success of any strategic planning process. They must be champions of the new vision. Their enthusiasm for the mission will be contagious and can rekindle in the congregation a renewed sense of purpose.

Momentum is essential in moving a congregation forward into a new future. You catch momentum by changing something and you sustain momentum by practicing certain practices over and over in excellent ways. You cannot create momentum but you can catch it. You can keep it for longer periods of time when you understand the wave. Jesus is right. You are not the wind. You are not the Spirit. However, if you learn more about the Spirit, you have a better chance of getting in its paths and pursuing it in effective ways.[13]

The Power of Purpose: Living into God's Kingdom of Care

One of the untold stories of servanthood is the witness of St. Paul's Episcopal Church located at Ground Zero in New York City. The congregation was the site of George Washington's first inaugural and has been engaged in ministry for over 200 years. On September 11, 2001 when the World Trade Towers collapsed there was damage to all the surrounding buildings except St. Paul. Located only a couple blocks away, it was discovered that not even one stained-glass window was cracked. God had a purpose for this church in this time of tragedy. It was to show an unwavering spirit by bringing hope and healing at Ground Zero.

St. Paul's opened its doors to become a place of rest and refuge for all the rescue workers. Today you can see evidence in the church of their ministry of hospitality and welcome. Through this act of service, they sought to restore bodies and souls. This revitalized the congregation and gave them a new sense of mission and purpose. Before 9/11 there may have been some uncertainty about their future in the city. Now they see clearly where God has led them into a new century of service and discipleship. Just as a new World Trade Tower has been built, so the people of St. Paul's have risen to the challenge of being God's servant church in New York City. Today they welcome thousands of pilgrims a week who still come to pray and to remember. They have come to know the truth of Jeremiah's words from the beginning of this chapter, and are living into God's future with hope.

Every faith community can aspire to be an expression of God's kingdom of care. Such spirit is captured well in the words of a powerful communion hymn written by Susan Briehl:

Send us now with faith and courage to the hungry, lost, bereaved.
In our living and our dying, we become what we receive:

Christ's own body. blessed and broken, cup o'erflowing, life outpoured, Given as a living token of your world redeemed, restored.[14]

The guiding principle for congregations seeking to create and implement a new vision for mission with a renewed sense of purpose is this: *understanding what it means to be a discipleship community in their own culture and context of care.* It means defining the effectiveness of their ministry not solely by what is taking place on the inside, but especially by what is happening outside the walls of the church. It is a vision that helps a congregation cultivate a culture of care and embrace what it means to partner with God in the care, healing, and redemption of the world. "Where love is stronger than hate, and where hope conquers despair" could be the vision statement of every gospel-centered community of care that seeks to help usher in the reign of God.

Questions for Reflection:

1. Why is vision so important to the vitality and health of a congregation?
2. What are the four stages of the strategic planning process?
3. How are vision and purpose interrelated?
4. What are some examples of change that a congregation needs to be aware of in mapping out a new vision for their future?
5. List a couple of key learnings from the section on the six steps of vision planning.

Notes

1. James A. Belasco and Ralph C. Stayer, *Flight of the Buffalo* (New York: Warner Books, 1993), 90.

2. Jo Ann Dollard, "Food Truck on the Move," from *Living Lutheran Stories* (Chicago: Evangelical Lutheran Church in America, 2014), 1–3.

3. Rick Rusaw and Eric Swanson, *The Externally Focused Church* (Loveland, CO: Group, 2004), 148.

4. Alan J. Roxburgh, *Missional Map-Making: Skills for Leading in Times of Transition* (San Francisco: Jossey-Bass, 2010), 82.

5. Anthony B. Robinson, *Changing the Conversation: A Third Way for Congregations* (Grand Rapids, MI: Eerdmans, 2008), 8.

6. Ibid., 120.

7. Gary Nelson, *Borderland Churches: A Congregation's Introduction to Missional Living* (St. Louis: Chalice, 2008), 96.

8. Ibid., 57.

9. Ibid., 19.

10. Darrell Guder, *Missional Church: A Vision for the Sending of the Church in North America* (Grand Rapids, MI: Eerdmans, 1998), 6.

11. Eric Swanson and Rick Rusaw, *The Externally Focused Church: Becoming the Best Church for the Community* (San Francisco: Jossey-Bass, 2010), 191.

12. Matthew 28:18 (paraphrased).

13. Bob Farr, *Renovate or Die: Ten Ways to Focus Your Church on Mission* (Nashville: Abingdon, 2011), 40.

14. Susan R. Briehl, "By Your Hand You Feed Your People", *Evangelical Lutheran Worship* (Minneapolis: Augsburg Fortress, 2006). Hymn 469. Text and Music © 2002 GIA Publications, Inc.

Appendix I

Bible Study

The Good Samaritan: A Parable of Care

Jesus' parable of the Good Samaritan as recorded in Luke 10:25-37 contains a message that is as contemporary and applicable today as it was in first-century Palestine. The story answers the question put to Jesus: "Who is my neighbor?" It suggests that whoever we discover is a person or persons in need, there we will find our neighbor. The twist that Jesus adds to this lesson is that it is a Samaritan—a clan of people often despised and viewed as suspect by Jewish religious leaders of the day—who is the real hero of the story. It is not one of their own; it is not a Levite, a teacher of the Law, nor is it a Priest. They both avoid the man who has been robbed and left for dead. It is left to a traveling Samaritan to bind up the victim's wounds and provide for his care, thus acting as the true neighbor. Below are some questions for group discussion or personal reflection.

Picture of The Good Samaritan by Chinese artist He Qi. www.heqiart.com.

1. What were some of the ways that the Good Samaritan was a good neighbor to the person who was in need?

2. Why do you think that the Levite and the Priest chose to avoid the man robbed and left for dead by walking on the other side of the road? Is there anything to justify their negligence for not assisting a person in need?

3. How is it that we are like the Priest or Levite in the story by "passing on the other side"?

4. What are some of the reasons that people of faith may pass and

not assist someone in need? Discuss the following and feel free to add to the list below:

a. Fear of getting involved and/or getting hurt.
b. Self-absorbed—not interested or able to see the needs of others.
c. Feeling inadequate to help or meet certain needs.
d. Preoccupied with dealing with one's own concerns.
e. Other:

5. How might the above categories describe reasons why congregations are not more active in providing community care and serving their neighbors in need?
6. Martin Luther once suggested that the best way to show our love for God is to care for the neighbor in need. How does this relate to the message of the Parable of the Good Samaritan?
7. Make a list of some of the people in your neighborhood or larger community who are in need. Consider what some of their specific needs and concerns might be.
8. What are some of the ways that you and your congregation could provide help to these neighbors in need?

Appendix II

A Missional Approach to Pastoral Care

Case Study Scenarios

PREMISE: You and your congregation represent Christ to those around you. You are the hands and feet of Jesus; you are the incarnation of a caring and loving God. As Mother Teresa once said: "We should not serve the poor because of Jesus, we should serve them because they ARE Jesus."

INSTRUCTIONS: Read the brief description of a community crisis listed below. 1) *What would be a pastoral care approach to responding to this crisis? 2) How might your congregation choose to get involved, if at all? 3) What would your role be?* Write a paragraph or two about your proposed plan of action that answers these questions for each scenario.

1. **COMMUNITY CENTER FIRE:** Several churches including your own support the local Community Service Center that houses various community services for the people of your town: e.g., WIC office, Training for the Unemployed, Financial Counseling, Marriage and Family Counseling, etc. While

serving all members of the community, the majority of people who use the services tend to be the poor and ethnic minorities. There has been a tragic fire that has destroyed much of the building and a number of offices. It is not clear how the fire started, though the Fire Marshall suspects arson; and it is not sure the building can be saved. Fortunately there is insurance on the building, but it may be at least a year before it can reopen.

2. **DEATH OF POPULAR STUDENT ATHLETE:** A member of your congregation is a popular football player at the local high school. He collapses on the field during practice and dies. The medical report reveals that he had a heart problem that the family physician had not detected. You know that many in the community, especially other students, will want to attend funeral services for the boy, but your sanctuary is small. Might you consider other venues? How will the community deal with their grief?

3. **TORNADO IN NEIGHBORING TOWN:** A devastating storm has razed many of buildings in the neighboring town, including the only ELCA church there. The congregation is without a worshiping facility and some church members and their neighbors have lost their homes and belongings.

4. **VANDALISM AT LOCAL FOOD BANK:** Your congregation has joined with other churches in town to organize a community food bank. Your members have faithfully helped provide money and food items, and some volunteer their service. Some rowdy teenagers have broken into the food bank and destroyed some food, smashed windows, and broken counters. It will take a number of volunteers and some funding to get the food bank up and running again.

Appendix III

Rites for Occasions of Special Transition Related to Children

Developed by Thomas H. Schattauer

Blessing of Parents during Pregnancy in Anticipation of Baptism

Dear friends: The expectation and birth of a child is at once a fearful, joyous, and solemn occasion in the life of a family. It is also an occasion for prayer and rejoicing in the Christian community. I bid you, therefore, to join these families in prayer and thanksgiving to Almighty God, the Lord of all life, for the gift of children expected and received.

The minister invites the assembly to pray for each set of expectant parents.

Let us pray for <u>name</u> and <u>name</u> and the child they have conceived. Almighty God, your wisdom abounds in the glory of creation and is beyond our understanding. Your love for us and all creatures is as gentle as a father's and as tender as a mother's. We give you thanks for creating new life and filling our hearts with joy and expectation. We proclaim your greatness and ask your sustaining care for these expectant parents and families and the little ones they await, that all of us may grow in wisdom and grace; through Jesus Christ our Savior and Lord.

Amen.

The minister blesses each set of expectant parents.

The Lord bless you and keep you, and bring you safely through your child's birth that you may find joy in this new life and bring your newborn to the waters of holy baptism.

Amen.

Thanksgiving for Children Given into Care (e.g., Adoption) and Blessing of Those Who Receive Them

Let us give thanks with *name(s)* for the gift of this child *name*, given into their care.

Let us pray for other children so received and for those who receive them.

God of love and mercy, protector and guardian of all, we give you thanks for this young child, *name*, and for the generosity of *name* and *name*, who have opened their arms and their home to her. Bless their household that they may find joy in their new life together. Make all such households places of laughter and love, of safety and security for the children received into care. May the love of caregivers so nurture and protect these children that they may heal and grow in body, mind, and spirit, through Jesus Christ our Savior and Lord, in whose name we pray.

Amen.

In hope and prayer that *name* may one day be brought to the waters of holy baptism, we offer the sign of the cross.

Name, receive the + cross on your forehead, a sign of God's endless love and mercy for you.

The Lord bless you and keep you all your days.

Amen.

Thanksgiving for the Birth/Adoption of a Child with Sign of Cross and Announcement of Baptism

The minister invites the assembly to give thanks for the birth or adoption of a child.

Let us give thanks with *name(s)* for the gift of *name* to be their son/daughter (and with *name(s)* for the gift of *his/her/their* new *sister/brother*).

God our creator, we give you thanks for new life begun among us in the gift of these children. Give their parents wisdom and patience, that they may cherish their children as your gift. As you will be pleased to receive them by the washing of Holy Baptism, so grant us grace to welcome them as heirs of your reign and members of the body of Christ; through the same Jesus Christ our Savior and Lord.

Amen.

The minister traces the cross on the forehead of each child.

Name, receive the + sign of the cross, a sign of God's endless love and mercy for you.

Amen.

The minister announces the time and place of the child's baptism.

Name will be baptized on *name of Sunday*, *date*, among the people of God at *name of congregation* [or] in this place.

The minister blesses the child and his/her family.

The Lord bless you and keep you in the promise of baptism.

Amen.

Prayers for Healing for Those Who Have Experienced Loss in Relation to Pregnancy and Childbirth

Dear friends: For many, there is significant loss and deep sorrow in loss of a pregnancy and in other circumstances related to pregnancy, childbirth, or the process of adoption. There are indeed many situations related to having children and not having children that call out for God's healing in our lives. This, too, is the occasion for prayer in the Christian community and for signs of solidarity with those who suffer. I bid you, therefore, to join in prayer to Almighty God, for all who know some form of anguish in this arena of life.

The minister invites the assembly to prayer for those who have suffered the loss of a pregnancy or a child at birth.

Let us pray for those in distress at the loss of *a pregnancy/child at birth*, including those we name in our hearts.

O God, who gathered Rachel's tears over her lost children, hear now the sorrow and distress of those who have suffered the loss of an expected child. In the darkness of loss, stretch out to them the strength of your arm and give them renewed assurance of your love; through your own suffering and risen Child Jesus.

Amen.

When individuals are present, the minister may lay both hands on the head of each parent, saying these words. The minister may also anoint their foreheads with oil, making the sign of the cross.

Name and _name_, in the name of our Savior Jesus Christ,

be strengthened and filled with God's grace,

that you may know the healing power of the Spirit.

Amen.

The minister invites the assembly to pray for anyone in the midst of loss.

Let us pray for any and all who have need of healing for whatever the loss or circumstance.

God of compassion, your Son Jesus Christ, the great physician, made the broken whole and healed the sick. Touch our wounds, relieve our hurts, and restore to us the wholeness of life, through the same Jesus Christ, our Savior and Lord.

Amen.

The minister concludes all of these prayers with a blessing over the entire assembly.

The Lord bless and keep us all in the promise of baptism within the communion of the church on the way of the cross until the day of Jesus Christ.

Amen.

The rites for blessing, thanksgiving, and healing in relation to pregnancy and birth have been developed by Thomas H. Schattauer for use in the Wartburg Seminary community, and are used here with his permission. The following sources have been consulted, used, and adapted.

Sources:

Evangelical Lutheran Worship: Pastoral Care (2008) and *Evangelical Lutheran Worship: Occasional Services for the Assembly* (2009). See "Preparing for baptism of infants or young children," "Signing with the cross in preparation for baptism," "Brief Order for Healing," "Healing and wholeness," "When a Child Dies before or at Birth," "During pregnancy," and "Birth of a child."

Evangelical Lutheran Worship (2006). See "Welcome to Baptism"; "Healing."

"The Preparation of Parents and Godparents for the Baptism of Infants and Young Children," *Book of Occasional Services—1994 edition (The Episcopal Church)*. This edition points to material in two other rites and suggests adaptations—"Blessing of a Pregnant Woman" in the 1994 edition and "Thanksgiving for the Birth or Adoption of a Child" in the *Book of Common Prayer* of 1979.

Occasional Services: A Companion to Lutheran Book of Worship (1982), p. 294, prayers #567 and #568.

Ramshaw, Gail. "Celebrating Baptism in Stages: A Proposal." *Alternative Futures for Worship.* Vol. 2: *Baptism and Confirmation.* Ed. Mark Searle. Liturgical Press, 1987, pp. 137–55.

Notes:

The signing with the cross is associated with the beginning of baptism in the catechumenal process; see "Welcome to Baptism" in *Evangelical Lutheran Worship.* In a congregation that regularly uses a full rite of baptismal welcome for all baptismal candidates, the prayer of thanksgiving for birth/adoption could be done in relation to such a rite.

Appendix IV

A Ministry Assessment Survey: The Seven Keys

A. Communication and Outreach

1. How is hospitality practiced by your congregation to make new people feel welcome?
2. What kind of technology is used to make worship "user friendly" (e.g., projection of songs and liturgy on a screen)?
3. Do you practice invitational evangelism (e.g., "Bring-a-friend Sunday")?
4. A congregation's website is the new front door to the church. What is done to make it attractive and informative and also up-to-date?
5. How are social media used to attract and follow up with new people (e.g., Facebook)?
6. How are new members assimilated into the church community?

B. Worship

1. Is there a clear focus on Word and Sacrament?
2. Do you practice "user friendly" worship—easy to follow?

3. Is there an evangelism focus to worship (communicate the gospel in ways that connect with the culture—e.g., multimedia, contemporary worship, etc.)?
4. Do people hear the "good news" in a way that inspires and can be applied to everyday life?

C. Campus/Facilities

1. Is most of your campus and facility accessible?
2. Do you practice good stewardship of your facility (e.g., multi-use of space, community groups, etc.)?
3. Do you have enough space or the "right" use of space?
4. Do you have adequate signage that provides directions for members and visitors?

D. Ministry Structure/Staffing

1. Are you structured to maintain the institution? Do you meet for the sake of meeting?
2. Do you minimize the meetings and maximize the ministry?
3. Are you staffed for growth?
4. Do you empower staff and volunteers to use their gifts (permission-giving ministry)?

E. Spiritual Formation & Disciple Making

1. Do members understand the importance of "being and making disciples" (living out the Great Commission)?
2. How do you prepare people for baptism and for baptismal living?
3. How intentional are you about the spiritual formation of congregational leaders? Do they understand their sense of call and vocation of being a missional leader?

4. Do you view your congregation as a center for equipping the baptized for ministry in daily life? If so, how do you do this?

F. Financial Viability and Sustainability

1. What is the state of the congregation's finances? a) healthy, b) sick, or c) in recovery
2. Are people being challenged to be "generous" disciples?
3. Do you have the financial resources you need to carry out your mission?

G. Clear Sense of Mission and Purpose

1. Do you think members understand what it means to be partners in God's mission?
2. Do staff, leaders, members have a compass (clear sense of purpose) to guide them?
3. How do you release the gifts of God's people in your congregation for God's mission?

Appendix V

Fifty Ways to Take Church to Your Community

Embrace an expansive concept of community.

1. Learn to regard your community as an extension of your congregation. A church's mission field goes beyond its membership to include all the people God calls it to serve. You are connected to individuals who never set foot in your building.
2. Know that what's happening within the church—preaching, worship, music, Bible study—is no longer enough to attract people in an age when church attendance is no longer a cultural expectation.
3. Don't sit in your church building waiting for people to come. Be prepared to meet people where they are.

Prepare spiritually.

4. Acknowledge the synergy between the Great Commandment in Matthew 22 (*love your neighbor as yourself*) and the Great Commission in Matthew 28 (*go and make disciples*). Evangelistic outreach expresses our love of others.
5. Remember that Jesus primarily engaged people through

everyday encounters, rather than in the Temple or synagogues. He fed people, met their everyday needs, and enjoyed the fellowship of others.

6. Express love and compassion for your community in big and small ways. Avoid judgmentalism.

7. Pray regularly for your neighbors and lift up community concerns.

8. Attend to the faith formation of existing members. Willingness to share faith and reach out to others develops as one grows in faith and discipleship.

9. Prepare spiritually for the transformation that creative, risk-taking outreach will bring.

Get to know the community surrounding your church.

10. Review demographic data from public, private, and denominational sources, but don't assume that statistics alone will tell the whole story.

11. Get out in your neighborhood. Walk the streets. Map the area, and record your observations. Note how the community is changing.

12. Assess community needs and assets. What are the needs of your context? Who are your neighbors, and how can you serve them?

13. Be attuned to where God is already at work in your community.

Listen and learn.

14. Know that ministries that truly bless a community often arise out of conversations where you listen for the hopes and dreams of people in your community.

15. Interview residents of the community. Sit in a park, diner, or

coffeehouse. Ask simply, "What are your challenges, hopes, longings, and dreams?"

16. Get to know the major public officials. They are people with tremendous influence. They need to know of your church's commitment to the community.

17. Involve many people from your church in this work. Hold one another accountable to the tasks of engaging and learning from others.

18. Discern clusters of issues and concerns that arise from these conversations. Ask what issues, suffering, injustices, or brokenness might you address.

Build authentic relationships.

19. Strive for meaningful engagement with others, not superficial gestures.

20. Make sure you are reaching out to people for the right reasons. If your motive is simply to get them to come to church, people will see right through to it.

21. Maintain appropriate boundaries, and respect all with whom you engage.

22. Collaborate with others who are also passionate about the community. Don't reinvent the wheel if you can partner with someone else serving the community.

Turn your existing ministries outward.

23. Challenge each church group with an inside focus to find a way to become involved with the community outside the church. A choir might sing at a nursing home, or trustees could sponsor a neighborhood cleanup.

24. Extend recruiting and advertising for church groups and events

to audiences beyond your congregation. For example, recruit for choir members in a local paper or community list serve.

25. Build relationships with those taking part in existing programs that serve the community, such as ELS classes, food pantry or clothes bank users, daycare families, etc.

Reach out through community events.

26. Plan "bridge events" designed explicitly to draw people from the community by providing for them something they need or enjoy—block parties, free concerts, seasonal events, parenting classes, sports camps, or school supply giveaways, etc. Source: *Get Their Name* by Bob Farr, Doug Anderson, and Kay Kotan (Abingdon, 2013).

27. Hold these events off church property or outside the church walls in venues where people feel comfortable and naturally congregate.

28. Get the word out through a well-planned publicity campaign.

29. Encourage church members to invite their friends and neighbors. It is less threatening for them to invite someone to a community event than to worship.

30. Avoid explicitly religious themes: no preaching, prayers, pressure, or financial appeals that might turn people off or reinforce negative stereotypes about church.

31. Remember, the event itself is not the purpose. The purpose is to meet people where they are and build relationships. Mingle. Get to know people.

32. Have a well-trained hospitality team. Make sure guests are enjoying themselves and know their attendance is appreciated.

33. Gathering people's names and information about them will permit follow-up to those for whom it is appropriate.

34. Invite those who attend community events to another event—sometimes called a "hand-off event"—planned to draw them into a deeper relationship.

Extend your congregation's spiritual presence beyond church walls.

35. Recognize that many "unchurched" people are spiritually inclined but apprehensive about attending church because they feel unwelcome, distrust institutions, or have been hurt in the past.
36. Pay attention to the heightened receptiveness to spiritual engagement around religious holidays such as Easter and Christmas.
37. Offer offsite worship services on special days, such as Christmas Eve, Palm Sunday, and Easter. Select familiar venues where people feel comfortable—parks, restaurants, parking lots, coffeehouses.
38. Offer imposition of ashes on Ash Wednesday in public places.
39. Partner with other institutions (such as nursing homes, hospitals, or prisons) or commercial establishments (restaurants, bars, shopping centers, or sports facilities) to offer worship services to their constituents or clientele on special days.
40. Plan creative outdoor events, such as live nativities or "blessing of the animals" services, to help make your church visibly present to the community in creative ways.
41. Hold your Vacation Bible School in a local park or recreation center. Canvass nearby neighborhoods to invite families.
42. Reach out to local media. Community outreach is often newsworthy, and reporters are often looking for religiously themed stories around the holidays.

Connect spiritual outreach to community service.

43. Acknowledge that many served through feeding and clothing ministries, justice ministries, weekday children's services, and other ministries of community service have no other connections with our churches.

44. Ask if these ministries inadvertently convey an "us and them" attitude or communicate that "you are not worthy of joining us."

45. Identify aspects of church life, such as characteristics of the building or how people dress, that may make some feel unwelcome. Are there alternatives that may reduce barriers for some to enter?

46. Treat everyone as a person of dignity who deserves respect.

47. Extend genuine hospitality to those you serve.

48. Focus first on building relationships of understanding and trust.

49. Consider adding a spiritual or discipleship element to community service activities but without any sense of expectation or requirement. For example, have a service or study following ESL classes for anyone interested.

50. Seek to conduct each activity in a way that connects people to God and the church.

"50 Ways to Take Church to the Community" is used by permission and was developed by the Lewis Center for Church Leadership at Wesley Theological Seminary as part of their "50 Ways to Build Strength" series. These documents provide tips for building strength in areas of ministry that are vital to church growth. They are available for free online at http://www.churchleadership.com/resources/50_ways_to_build_strength.htm. The Lewis Center's free online newsletter is available at www.churchleadership.com.

Bibliography

Adams, Mark, with Minerva Carcano, Gerald Kicanas, Kirk Smith, and Stephen Talmage. *Bishops on the Border: Pastoral Responses to Immigration.* New York: Morehouse, 2013.

Anderson, Gerbert, and Edward Foley. *Mighty Stories, Dangerous Rituals: Weaving Together the Human and the Divine.* San Francisco: Jossey-Bass, 1998.

Barger, Rick. *A New and Right Spirit: Creating an Authentic Church in a Consumer Culture.* Herndon, VA: Alban Institute, 2005.

Bouman, Stephen. *The Mission Table: Renewing Congregation and Community.* Minneapolis: Augsburg Fortress, 2013.

Brown, Cherie R., and George J. Mazza. *Leading Diverse Communities: A How-To Guide for Moving from Healing into Action.* San Francisco: Jossey-Bass, 2005.

Coyle, Suzanne M. *Uncovering Spiritual Narratives: Using Story in Pastoral Care and Ministry.* Minneapolis: Fortress Press, 2014.

Cunningham, Sarah. *Portable Faith: How to Take Your Church to the Community.* Nashville: Abingdon, 2013.

Daubert, Dave, and Amy Walter-Peterson. *Building Healthy Communities Together: A Framework for Area Ministry Strategy in the Evangelical Lutheran Church in America.* Chicago: Evangelical Lutheran Church in America, 2014.

Doehring, Carrie. *The Practice of Pastoral Care: A Postmodern Approach.* Louisville: Westminster John Knox, 2006.

DuBois, Dwight. *The Scattering: Imagining a Church that Connects Faith and Life.* Eugene: Wipf & Stock, 2015.

Duckworth, Jessicah. *Wide Welcome: How the Unsettling Presence of Newcomers Can Save the Church.* Minneapolis: Augsburg Fortress, 2013.

Everist, Norma C., and Craig L. Nessan. *Transforming Leadership: New Vision for a Church in Mission.* Minneapolis: Augsburg Fortress, 2008.

Farr, Bob. *Renovate or Die: Ten Ways to Focus Your Church on Mission.* Nashville: Abingdon, 2008.

Foss, Michael. *Real Faith for Real Life: Living the Six Marks of Discipleship.* Minneapolis: Augsburg Fortress, 2004.

_____. *Reviving the Congregation: Pastoral Leadership in a Changing Context.* Minneapolis: Augsburg Fortress, 2014.

Gunderson, Gary. *Deeply Woven Roots: Improving the Quality of Life in Your Community.* Minneapolis: Fortress Press, 1997.

Heifetz, Ronald. *Leadership Without Easy Answers.* Cambridge, MA: Harvard University Press, 1998.

Heifetz, Ronald, and Marty Linsky. *The Practice of Adaptive Leadership: Tools and Tactics for Chaging Your Organization and the World.* Boston: Harvard Business Publishing, 2009.

Hoeft, Jeanne, L. Shannon Jung, and Joretta Marshall. *Practicing Care in Rural Congregations and Communities.* Minneapolis: Augsburg Fortress, 2013.

Hoffman, Paul E. *Faith Forming Faith: Bringing New Christians to Baptism and Beyond.* Eugene, OR: Cascade, 2012.

Hunsinger, Deborah van Deusen, and Theresa Latini. *Transforming Church Conflict: Compassionate Leadership in Action.* Louisville: Westminster John Knox, 2013.

Hunter, Joel C. *Church Distributed: How the Church Can Thrive in the Coming Era of Connection.* Longwood, FL: Distributed Church Press. 2007.

Jacobsen, Dennis A. *Doing Justice: Congregations and Community Organizing.* Minneapolis: Fortress Press, 2001.

Kegan, Robert, and Lisa Laskow Lahey. *Immunity to Change: How to*

Overcome It and Unlock the Potential in Yourself and Your Organization. Boston: Harvard Business Press, 2009.

Kornfeld, Margaret Zipse. *Cultivating Wholeness: A Guide to Care and Counseling in Faith Communities.* New York: Continuum, 1998.

Lartey, Emmanuel. *In Living Color: An Intercultural Approach to Pastoral Care and Counseling.* London: Jessica Kingsley, 2003.

Lathrop, Gordon W. *Holy People: A Liturgial Ecclesiology.* Minneapolis: Fortress Press, 2006.

Laubach, David C. *Twelve Steps to Congregational Transformation: A Practical Guide for Leaders.* Valley Forge, PA: Judson, 2006.

Latini, Theresa. *The Church and the Crisis of Community: A Practical Theology of Small Group Ministry.* Grand Rapids, MI: Eerdmans, 2011.

McClure, Barbara J. *Moving Beyond Individualism in Pastoral Care and Counseling: Reflections on Theory, Theology, and Practice.* Cambridge: Lutterworth, 2011.

Minatrea, Milfred. *Shaped by God's Heart: The Passion and Practices of Missional Churches.* San Francisco: Jossey-Bass, 2004.

Morse, Rick. *From Our Doorsteps: Developing a Ministry Plan That Makes Sense.* St. Louis: Chalice, 2010.

Nelson, Gary. *Borderland Churches: A Congregation's Introduction to Missional Living.* St. Louis: Chalice, 2008.

Nessan, Craig. *Beyond Maintenance to Mission: A Theology of the Congregation.* Minneapolis: Augsburg Fortress, 2010.

Niringiye, David Zac. *The Church: God's Pilgrim People.* Downers Grove: Inter Varsity Press, 2015.

Purnell, Douglas. *Conversations as Ministry: Stories and Strategies for Confident Caregiving.* Cleveland: Pilgrim, 2003.

Ramshaw, Elaine. *Ritual and Pastoral Care.* Philadelphia: Fortress Press, 1987.

Robinson, Anothony B. *Changing the Conversation: A Third Way for Congregations.* Grand Rapids, MI: Eerdmans, 2008.

———. *Transforming Congregational Culture.* Grand Rapids, MI: Eerdmans, 2003.

Rouse, Rick, and Craig Van Gelder. *A Field Guide for the Missional*

Congregation: Embarking on a Journey of Transformation. Minneapolis: Augsburg Fortress, 2008.

Rouse, Richard W. *Fire of Grace: The Healing Power of Forgiveness*. Minnneapolis: Augsburg Fortress, 2005.

Roxburgh, Alan. *Missional Map-Making: Skills for Leading in Times of Transition*. San Francisco: Jossey-Bass, 2010.

————. *Missional: Joining God in the Neighborhood*. Grand Rapids, MI: Baker, 2011.

Roxburgh, Alan, and Fred Romanuk. *The Missional Leader: Equipping Your Church to Reach a Changing World*. San Francisco: Jossey-Bass, 2006.

Rusaw, Rick, and Eric Swanson. *The Externally Focused Church*. Loveland, CO: Group, 2004.

Schmalzle, Robert, with Aaron Schmalzle. *The 7 Habits of Jesus: A Faith Formation Handbook for Discipleship*. Kissimmee, FL: New Life Publishing, 2014.

Smith, Daniel P., and Mary K. Sellon. *Pathyway to Renewal: Practical Steps for Congregations*. Lanham, MD: Rowman & Littlefield, 2008.

Smith, Susan Marie. *Caring Liturgies: The Pastoral Power of Christian Ritual*. Minneapolis: Augsburg Fortress, 2012.

Stairs, Jean. *Listening for the Soul: Pastoral Care and Spiritual Direction*. Minneapolis: Augsburg Fortress, 2000.

Stevenson-Moessner, Jeanne. *A Primer in Pastoral Care*. Minneapolis: Fortress Press, 2005.

Swanson, Eric, and Rick Rusaw. *The Externally Focused Quest: Becoming the Best Church for the Community*. San Francisco: Jossey-Bass, 2010.

Switzer, David K. *Pastoral Care Emergenices*. Minneapolis: Fortress Press, 2000.

Taylor, Charles. *The Skilled Pastor: Counseling as the Practice of Theology*. Minneapolis: Fortress Press, 1991.

Van Engen, Charles. *God's Missionary People: Rethinking the Purpose of the Local Church*. Grand Rapids: Baker, 1991.

Wiener, Nancy H., and Jo Hirschmann. *Maps and Meaning: Levitical Models for Contemporary Care*. Minneapolis: Fortress Press, 2014.

Wimberly, Edward P. *Recalling Our Own Stories: Spiritual Renewal for Religious Caregivers*. San Francisco: Jossey-Bass, 1997.

Woolever, Cynthia, and Deborah Bruce. *Places of Promise: Finding Strength in Your Congregation's Location*. Louisville: Westminster John Knox, 2008.

Zscheile, Dwight, ed. *Cultivating Sent Communities: Missional Spiritual Formation*. Grand Rapids, MI: Eerdmans, 2012.

Index of References

Index of Names and Subjects